TED KENNEDY

The Dream That Never Died

Also by Edward Klein

TED KENNEDY

The Dream That Never Died

EDWARD KLEIN

CROWN PUBLISHERS

NEW YORK

CROWN and the Crown colophon are registered
trademarks of Random House, Inc.

Library of Congress Cataloging-in-Publication Data
is available upon request.

ISBN 978-0-307-45103-3

Printed in the United States of America

Design by Barbara Sturman

10 9 8 7 6 5 4 3 2 1

First Edition

For Dolores

This time for providing the missing chip

FOR ALL THOSE whose cares have been our concern, the work goes on, the cause endures, the hope still lives, and the dream shall never die.

—EDWARD M. KENNEDY[1]

Contents

Author's Note

METAMORPHOSIS

———

Let others delight in the good old days;
I am delighted to be alive right now.
This age is suited to my way of life.

—OVID[1]

ON A FINE summer's day in 1970, Ted Kennedy skippered his sailboat from Hyannis Port over to Monhegan Island, an unspoiled, rocky outcropping ten miles off the coast of Maine, where I customarily spent the month of August with my children. He'd come to visit our mutual friend, the artist Jamie Wyeth, who'd painted a portrait of Ted's brother Jack not long after the president's assassination. Jamie always worked from live subjects, and while making his preliminary sketches of JFK, he'd asked Ted to sit in, as it were, for the dead president. As the portrait took shape, Ted had assumed the identity of his martyred brother, and in that guise, he and Jamie had become fast friends.

Ted and Joan Kennedy were staying with Jamie and his wife, Phyllis, who owned the most beautiful home on the island. It had once belonged to the famous illustrator Rockwell Kent, and it overlooked a boulder-strewn beach called Lobster Cove, where a picturesque old shipwreck lay rusting on its side.

Automobiles weren't permitted on Monhegan Island, and I ran into the Kennedys and Wyeths as they were coming down the footpath from Lobster Cove on their way to the general store. Phyllis Wyeth, who'd been left paralyzed from the waist down as the result of an accident, was in a wheelchair. She introduced me to her weekend guests: Joan, thirty-three, blond and willowy, at the height of her mature beauty; and Ted, thirty-eight, in robust good health. It was easy to see why Ted had been called the handsomest of the handsome Kennedy brothers.

"How are you, Senator," I said, shaking his hand.

My commonplace greeting seemed to perturb him, perhaps because Phyllis had mentioned that I was a journalist with *Newsweek*, and Ted Kennedy, at that time, was a fugitive from the media. Recently, Massachusetts had released the official transcript of the inquest into the 1969 death of Mary Jo Kopechne on Chappaquiddick Island. The judge presiding over the inquest strongly implied that a drunken Ted Kennedy had been driving Mary Jo to a sexual tryst when his car plunged off a bridge and into a body of water, where Mary Jo died.

I couldn't tell whether Ted had a sailor's sunburn, or whether his face was scarlet with shame. His edgy defensiveness was underscored by his stumbling syntax—a stammer that at times made him sound slow-witted and even a bit dumb.

"Well, um, yes, ah, glorious day . . ." he said. "Beautiful here, isn't it? . . . Sailing, um. . . . Good day . . . er, for that. . . . Wind. . . ."

Someone once referred to Ted Kennedy's off-the-cuff speaking style—as opposed to his superbly crafted speeches—as a "parody of [Yankees manager] Casey Stengel: nouns in search of verbs."[2] I later learned that the senator was aware of his tendency to speak in cryptic fragments, joking that as the youngest of nine children, he'd never had a chance to complete a sentence.[3] To correct the problem, he'd consulted a psychologist, who prescribed a daily therapeutic regimen to make him sound more intelligible when he wasn't using a prepared text. But he quickly lost interest in the therapy, and kept on *uh*-ing and *ah*-ing with no noticeable improvement.[4]

As we talked, I was struck by the fact that Ted didn't look at Joan. Their eyes never met. Indeed, they didn't even bother with the casual intimacies that are common between husband and wife.

Although I didn't know it at the time, Joan was well on her way to becoming a full-blown alcoholic. If Ted had once counted on Joan to turn a blind eye to his infidelities, her alcoholism had changed all that. Instead of tranquilizing her and making her more submissive, drink had freed Joan to speak her mind.

She had recently given an indiscreet interview to the *Ladies' Home Journal.* She and Ted, she said, "know our good and bad traits, we have seen one another at rock bottom. . . ."[5] It was clear that Joan's tendency to talk about Ted in less than glowing terms had put a strain on their marriage. The tragedy of Chappaquiddick had only made matters worse.

AFTER OUR BRIEF chat on Monhegan Island, ten years passed before I ran into Ted Kennedy again. This time, it was at a Christmas party given by his sister-in-law Jacqueline Kennedy Onassis at her Fifth Avenue penthouse apartment. Ted was still recovering from his ill-fated primary race against President Jimmy Carter. A month or so before Jackie's cocktail reception, Carter had been soundly defeated by Ronald Reagan in the general election, which must have given Ted Kennedy a feeling of schadenfreude. It also might have accounted for the high spirits he displayed that December evening at Jackie's.

Ted had gained a good deal of weight, and there were strands of gray in his thick mass of disordered hair. I had heard rumors that he and Joan were living apart, and in fact he'd come to the party without her. Joan's absence was particularly conspicuous because other members of Jackie's extended family—including her mother, her stepbrother, and assorted Kennedys, Shrivers, Lawfords, and Smiths—were present. So were a few favored writers and journalists who, like me, had been befriended by Jackie.

"Teddy," Jackie said as she introduced us, "this is Ed Klein. He used to be at *Newsweek*, and now he's the editor of the *New York Times Magazine*."

"The senator and I have met before," I said. "You were visiting Jamie and Phyllis Wyeth on Monhegan Island."

"Oh, yes, um, I remember that, ah, day, ah, well," he said.

But he was slurring his words and speaking more loudly than necessary, and I concluded that he'd had too much to drink. Still, it was interesting to note that, even when inebriated, Ted Kennedy displayed impeccable manners. He had not yet turned fifty and could still hold his liquor.

AGAIN, A DECADE or so went by before I met Ted Kennedy for the third time. It was the early 1990s, and I'd left the *Times* after eleven years as editor of its Sunday magazine and was now writing for *Vanity Fair* and *Parade*. I'd been invited as the sole journalist to attend a private dinner given by a group of wealthy contributors in honor of Senator Kennedy at the "21" Club, a Manhattan mecca for top business executives and Wall Street bankers.

Ted was preparing for a reelection campaign, and although he'd established a record as one of the Senate's all-time greats (he'd had a hand in passing every major health, education, and civil rights bill over the past thirty years), he was in serious political trouble back home in Massachusetts. As a result of his entanglement in the sordid Palm Beach rape case against his nephew William Kennedy Smith, Ted's poll numbers had sunk to an all-time low. It looked as though the unthinkable might happen: a Kennedy might actually lose a race in Massachusetts.

He loved the Senate, and he intended to fight with every weapon at his disposal to keep his seat. His father, Joseph P. Kennedy, had once famously said: "Politics is like war. It takes three things to win. The first is money and the second is money and the third is money."[6] Ted Kennedy had come to that night's dinner to raise a lot of money.

He was now sixty years old, and when he entered the room, I hardly recognized him. There, in the middle of his creased and crumpled face, was his alcohol-ravaged nose—a rough, veined protuberance that was as gnarled as the knot of an oak tree. His bloated body was bursting at the armpits of his suit jacket.

He was seated at a big round table next to his attractive new wife, Victoria Reggie Kennedy, a tall, dark-haired, hazel-eyed woman who was twenty-two years his junior. Vicki glowed with vigor and self-confidence. A successful lawyer in her own right, Vicki had a way of inserting herself into the conversation without appearing to upstage the senator. In fact, it soon became apparent that Vicki was there to look after Ted, monitor his answers, adjust them if necessary, add some nuances—and make sure that he didn't drink too much. She sent the waiter away when he attempted to fill her husband's wineglass for the third time. Ted seemed perfectly content to let Vicki run the show.

His speaking disability was on full display that evening. He had trouble answering the simplest questions. He talked in sentence fragments and at times didn't make much sense. Each time he faltered, he'd look over at Vicki, who'd beam back at him, and each time he seemed to draw renewed confidence from her. I couldn't help but notice the submissive way he related to Vicki, and compare that with the cool indifference he'd shown Joan on Monhegan Island some twenty years before.

By the end of the evening, I'd come to an extraordinary conclusion: This was no longer the same Ted Kennedy I had first met on Monhegan Island. *This* Ted Kennedy was a less agitated, restless, and fretful man; he was also less self-conscious and ill at ease, less vain and egocentric.

Fundamental change in a person of Ted Kennedy's age is rare. But here was living proof that it was possible. There could be no mistaking the fact that the remote and unresponsive Ted Kennedy of Monhegan Island—the *fugitive* Ted Kennedy—had morphed into someone else. He seemed like a more fully developed human being.

What, I wondered, accounted for this remarkable transformation?

THAT QUESTION HAS never been far from my mind in the years following the "21" Club dinner. Since then, I've written a half dozen books, including three about the life and death of Jacqueline Kennedy Onassis and one about the tragic history of the Kennedy family titled *The Kennedy Curse*. As I delved deeply into the massive literature on the Kennedy family and interviewed hundreds of their friends and associates, I noted that Ted Kennedy's metamorphosis was hardly ever scrutinized in the thousands of words that have been written about him. He was, I concluded, the least understood and the most underappreciated Kennedy of them all.

And so, when he came out for Barack Obama—marshaling the legendary power of the Kennedy name to help boost Obama's presidential candidacy—I decided to devote a book to Ted Kennedy. At the time, he hadn't been diagnosed with incurable brain cancer. He still planned to run for reelection in 2012, when he would be eighty years old. But after his brain surgery, he had to confront the somber prospect that he wouldn't be around to serve another term in the Senate.

That realization must have been the cruelest blow of all. For the Senate had come to define Ted Kennedy even more than his famous last name. An unabashed liberal, he had many things he still hoped to accomplish—rights to be protected, wrongs to be redressed. But he had a particularly aggressive form of brain cancer, and he knew that he was running out of time.

Since his brain surgery in June 2008, each day had been a reprieve; each week a miracle. And when those weeks had turned into months, his family and doctors were astounded by his resilience, as was the entire country. All Americans, including those who did not agree with his liberal politics, were in awe of his gallant last stand. He was no longer sitting in for his dead brother. He had become his own portrait in courage.

PART ONE

"There Are More of Us
Than Trouble"

———

1

Washington, D.C., April 6, 1953

T RAIN NO. 173, the *Federal Express*, hurtled through the night at nearly seventy miles an hour. Tucked away in the swaying Pullman sleeping car was the youngest member of the Kennedy clan, Edward Moore Kennedy—"Eddie" to his sisters, "Teddy" to his brothers, "Ted" to the rest of the world. He was an exceptionally handsome young man, just turned twenty-one, with a mane of glistening hair, the trademark Kennedy teeth, and the build of an athlete. At six foot two and two hundred pounds, he barely fit into the narrow Pullman bed, and at each bend and curve along the way, he had to hold on to the bed railing to prevent himself from falling out of his berth.

The *Federal Express* chased the ghostly beam of its headlamps through Boston, Providence, New Haven, New York, Philadelphia, Wilmington, and Baltimore. After the Baltimore Yards, the engineer notched the controller up to eighty miles an hour for the run into Washington, D.C. When the train reached signal number 1339, about two miles from Union Station, Ted finally found the sleep that had eluded him for the past several hours.

He was groggy as he stepped off the train onto Track 16 a few minutes before 7:00 A.M. He grabbed his suitcase and made his way down the deserted sidewalks of Delaware Avenue to the Senate Office Building. He was something of an architecture buff, and the simple majesty of the building impressed him. Inside, twin marble staircases led from the rotunda to an entablature and coffered dome. The great space was empty except for a lone guard asleep behind the security desk. Ted didn't disturb him as he set out in search of Room 362, his brother Jack's new office.

"I can remember the first time I ever visited there," he recalled many years later. "It was back in 1953 and I was a schoolboy. My brother John had just been elected to the Senate. I'd come down to visit him on the night train. Getting in early, I arrived at his office at about seven thirty in the morning. No one was there. So I sat down on my suitcase out in the hall.

"Next door was the office of the vice president, and just then Nixon came along,"* Ted continued. "He introduced himself and invited me into his office. It was the first time I'd ever met him. We had a pleasant talk, sparring about who got in first in the morning and that sort of thing."[1]

. . .

---

*In his constitutional duty as presiding officer of the Senate, where he has the power to cast a tiebreaking vote, the vice president keeps an office in a Senate office building.

. . .

JACK KENNEDY SHOWED up a little before nine o'clock. The Kennedy brothers had not seen much of each other in quite some time. Jack had been busy running for the Senate—his launching pad for the White House—while Ted had been getting himself into trouble. At the end of his freshman year at Harvard, he was suspended for hiring a student to take his final Spanish exam. When his father found out about it, he went ballistic. Ted knew how to blarney his father; he explained that in order to play football at Harvard, you had to demonstrate a proficiency in a foreign language, and knowing how important it was to his father that he make the team, he had cheated on the test.

"From then on [my father] was calm," Ted said. "It was just 'How can we help you?' and he never brought up the subject again."[2]

Harvard's longtime president James Bryant Conant made it clear that Ted could seek readmission after an appropriate time had elapsed, and Joseph Kennedy immediately began a campaign to get his son back in the college's good graces. But war had broken out in Korea, and Ted saw a chance to atone for his disgrace by enlisting in the army. Thanks to his father's influence, Ted served his two-year stint far from the front lines, as a private first class in the military police in Europe. He was in France when he heard the news that Jack had won a come-from-behind victory over Massachusetts's senior senator, Henry Cabot Lodge.

From Paris, Teddy whipped off a congratulatory telegram:

IL EST FATIGUE ET TRISTE SES YEUX SONT ROUGE CE QUE VOUS FEISIEZ [SIC] A LODGE NE DEVRAIT PAS ARRIVER AUX MORTS =TED ("HE IS TIRED AND SAD HIS EYES ARE RED WHAT YOU WERE DOING TO LODGE SHOULDN'T HAPPEN TO THE DEAD. TED")[3]

Ted's telegrams were collector's items. He once telegraphed his father:

HAPPY FATHERS DAY HAVING BARRELS OF FUN SEND MONEY
FOR MORE BARRELS LOVE = TED[4]

He inherited his love of verbal jousting from the Fitzgeralds, his mother's side of the family. The youngest of nine, Ted was doted on by his grandfather, John Francis "Honey Fitz" Fitzgerald, the former mayor of Boston and an Irish politician of the old school. As they strolled down the streets of Boston, Ted would watch—and learn—as Honey Fitz greeted everyone with a vigorous handshake or, in the case of pretty young women, with an effusive hug.

"When I was going to school," Ted recalled, "I'd get Sunday lunch off and I'd go on into the Bellevue Hotel and have Sunday lunch with [Grandpa] . . . and he would take you all through the kitchen and introduce you to all of the waitresses. On several occasions, I remember [Bobby] was there—and he would join us. And then in the afternoon he'd take us for a walk through the Boston Common and we'd go down to the Old North Church and sit outside in a chair and look up at the steeple and view the architecture. . . . Once in a while we'd start out the door to go and view these various historic sights and he'd get wrapped up in conversation with friends and we'd never get there. . . . I heard my first off-color story from Grandpa. He was laughing so hard."[5]

ALONE WITH JACK in his small office, Ted got his first good look at his brother. He was pleasantly surprised by Jack's appearance. For years, their father had gone to great lengths to cover up the fact that Jack suffered from several serious medical conditions, including Addison's disease, a sometimes fatal malady that was caused by inadequate secretion of hormones by the adrenal cortex. Joe Kennedy feared that if the truth got out, it would sabotage Jack's political career.

"Each health problem was treated as a political problem, to be *spun*," wrote Chris Matthews. "[Jack] had developed, in fact, a reliable smoke screen. When he needed crutches, it was because of the 'wartime injury.' When he turned yellow or took sick because of Addison's disease, it was billed as a recurrence of malaria, another reminder of wartime service."[6]

The newly sworn-in senator had gained some needed flesh; he weighed a hundred and sixty pounds—about fifteen pounds more than his average for the past five years.[7] The whites of his eyes weren't yellowed from jaundice, indicating that he had his Addison's disease under control. And he didn't need to use crutches for his chronic bad back.

But if Ted was impressed by Jack's appearance, he didn't think much of his brother's office. It consisted of three tiny windowless rooms—one for the new senator; another for his chief of staff and administrative assistant, Ted Reardon, and his legislative assistant, Ted Sorensen; and a third for Evelyn Lincoln, his personal secretary, and a pool of secretaries and unpaid assistants who answered constituent mail.[8]

"Kennedy worked at a furious pace," noted biographer Michael O'Brien. "Many mornings he was bursting with new ideas. 'I have several things for you to do,' he would say to [Evelyn Lincoln] as soon as he entered his office. 'First . . . Second . . . Third . . .' While dictating letters, he would pace back and forth or swing a golf club at an imaginary ball. He insisted mail got immediate attention.

Helen Lempart, one of his secretaries, said everyone had to make up a folder saying how many pieces of mail came in, how many were answered, and what the backlog was. There was a constant tracking of people in and out."[9]

The hallway between Jack's office in Room 362 and Richard Nixon's in Room 361 was busy all day long. "The two of them were continuously tripping over cameras," recalled Evelyn Lincoln. "You couldn't get through. Hardly a day went by, when Nixon was in Washington, that all kinds of cameras and press equipment were not lined up outside his door."[10]

Despite Nixon's later reputation as a politician who had a kind of Hatfield-McCoy feud with the TV camera, he was actually far ahead of his colleagues in his sophisticated grasp of the power of television.[11] Jack Kennedy was so impressed by Nixon's exploitation of the new medium that he made a point of telling his brother Ted about it.

After the *New York Post* revealed that Nixon had been the beneficiary of a secret "rich men's" slush fund, Nixon fell into danger of being dumped by Dwight Eisenhower as his vice-presidential running mate. To save his job, Nixon went on television and gave his famous "Checkers speech"—a demagogic appeal that involved the family dog, Checkers. As a result of that speech, millions of telegrams poured into Republican National Committee headquarters imploring Eisenhower to keep Nixon on the ticket.[12]

As far as Ted could tell, Jack and Dick Nixon seemed to have a mutual admiration society. "One reason for the across-the-hall cordiality," wrote Chris Matthews, "was that while Kennedy and his staff assumed even back then that the 1960 Republican presidential nomination was Nixon's to lose, the vice president had little reason to suspect Kennedy as a rival. . . . By all outward appearances,

[Kennedy] seemed a genial dilettante destined for a long, no-heavy-lifting career in the Senate. . . ."[13]

Nixon was not the only one who sold Jack Kennedy short. When Ted Sorensen told friends that he was interviewing for a job with the new senator, they warned him against taking it. "Kennedy's commitment to civil liberties, New Deal spending, church-state separation, and civil rights was uncertain; and his closeness to his famously conservative father gave [my friends] pause," Sorensen explained. ". . . Senator Kennedy wouldn't hire anyone his father wouldn't hire, and . . . Ambassador Kennedy had hired only Irish Catholics."[14]

But Jack's stunning victory over Lodge in the 1952 election had elevated him to the status of a political comer. He had managed to defeat an incumbent Republican in a year when the Republicans swept the White House, the Senate, and the House. He was featured in magazines, and was sought after by the new medium of television.

"When he walked into a room, he became its center," Ted Sorensen recalled. "When he spoke, people stopped and listened. When he grinned, even on television, viewers smiled back at him. He was much the same man in private as he was in public. It was no act—the secret of his magic appeal was that he had no magic at all. But he did have charisma. . . . It had to be experienced to be believed. It wasn't only his looks or his words; it was a special lightness of manner, the irony, the teasing, the self-effacement, the patient 'letting things be.' Although he could be steely and stern when frustrated, he never lost his temper. When times were bad, he knew they would get better—when they were good, he knew they could get worse."[15]

Jack bore an uncanny resemblance to Lord Melbourne, a

nineteenth-century British prime minister who was the subject of his favorite biography, *The Young Melbourne*, by David Cecil. Like Melbourne, Jack "thought poorly of the world, but enjoyed every moment of it."[16] Biographer Cecil might have had Jack in mind when he wrote of Lord Melbourne: "He had the family zest for life, their common sense, their animal temperament. But some chance of heredity . . . had infused into this another strain, finer, and more unaccountable. His mind showed it. It was not just that he was cleverer than his brothers and sisters; but his intelligence worked on different lines, imaginative, disinterested, questioning. It enjoyed thought for its own sake, it was given to curious speculations, that had no reference to practical results."[17]

JACK HAD A better mind than Ted, and Ted knew it. Once, Ted confessed to the historian Arthur Schlesinger Jr.: "I've been trying to read that list of books which Jack said were his favorites. Could he really have enjoyed those books? I tried to read Bemis on John Quincy Adams and Allan Nevins on the coming of the Civil War, and I just couldn't get through them."[18]

But in many other ways, Ted surpassed his brother. For one thing, Ted was taller and far handsomer than Jack. And Ted's prowess on the football field earned Jack's praise and envy. "[W]hile Ted was not what I would call a natural athlete," said Henry Lamar, his football coach at Harvard, "he was an outstanding player, the kind that carried out his assignments to the letter. . . . I've never seen any of [the Kennedy brothers] really excited, but Teddy, in particular, would respond to a hard knock by playing harder. . . . He was that kind of kid. The harder you played against him, the harder he'd play against you."[19]

And there was yet another difference between the brothers.

Ted was the one who most closely resembled his grandfather, the fun-loving and gregarious Honey Fitz. If Ted did not have a first-rate mind, he had a first-rate political temperament. Jack readily conceded that Ted was the best politician in the family.

But perhaps the biggest difference between the two brothers was in the way they viewed public service. A pragmatist at heart, Jack did not look upon government as a means of promoting an ideology. Like his hero, Lord Melbourne, he believed the world was ruled mainly by "folly, vanity, and selfishness,"[20] and there was not much that government could—or should—do about it. By contrast, Ted was deeply troubled by the plight of the less fortunate. Although at this stage of his life he was still trying to formulate a coherent political philosophy, he was on his way to becoming a tribune of the powerless, the persecuted, and the downtrodden.

"His induction into the army as an enlisted man exposed him firsthand, in a way none of his naval officer brothers had experienced, to the fact that many people, especially blacks, came from severely disadvantaged backgrounds, and that so much of what he had taken for granted all his life was utterly foreign to them and, moreover, forever unattainable by them," wrote Joe McGinniss in his 1993 study of Ted, *The Last Brother*.[21]

Another biographer, Ralph G. Martin, came to the same conclusion in his 1995 Kennedy family history, *Seeds of Destruction: Joe Kennedy and His Sons*. "All his life, Teddy had lived in a privileged cocoon," Martin wrote. "He had been cloistered, insulated. Private schools, tennis, sailing, parties. Suddenly [in the army] he was scraping food off metal trays and sleeping in a barrack with young men who spoke a different language of a different world. It was probably one of the most important experiences that had ever happened to him. It would redirect his life into a real world."[22]

After his two-year hitch in the army, Ted was discharged in

March 1953. He was readmitted to Harvard but had several months to kill before returning to college in the fall. In the meantime, he told Jack, he planned to volunteer as a basketball coach with underprivileged black and Puerto Rican kids in Boston's tough South End neighborhood.[23]

2

———

M<small>ANY OF THE</small> differences between Ted and Jack could be traced to the fact that they were almost fifteen years apart in age and had had strikingly different childhood experiences. Jack had been a frail boy with an intellectual bent; he spent a great deal of time reading in bed while recovering from a variety of illnesses. By contrast, Ted had been a robust and healthy child who displayed little intellectual curiosity. As the baby of the family, he was doted on by his older sisters. Jack's childhood illnesses were so life threatening that he grew up believing he was living on borrowed time. Ted grew up feeling immune to the laws that govern other people, and somehow divinely protected from the inevitable consequences of his deeds and misdeeds.

Yet a series of family traumas helped forge an extremely close bond between the two brothers. In the 1940s, three of their siblings—Rosemary, Joseph P. Kennedy Jr., and Kathleen—met tragic fates.

In 1941, their father had his mentally disabled, twenty-three-year-old daughter Rosemary lobotomized, because her uncontrollable behavior and sexual acting out threatened to ruin his plans to put a son in the White House. At the time, Jack was a twenty-four-year-old and about to become a naval officer. He heard about Rosemary's tragic fate but was not around to witness it in person. Ted, on the other hand, was an impressionable nine-year-old boy attending prep school who lived through the family trauma.

The lobotomy—a barbaric procedure that consists of cutting the connections to and from the prefrontal cortex of the brain—was botched, and Rosemary was reduced to a life of incontinence and incoherent babble. She was sent to live at St. Coletta, an institution for the retarded, in Jefferson, Wisconsin, where she died, at the age of eighty-six, in 2005.

In later years, Ted would say that Rosemary's plight inspired him to make health care one of his chief political causes.[1] But before he entered public life, Rosemary's ghost was a persistent and disturbing presence. Her mysterious disappearance was a forbidden topic in the Kennedy household. When young Teddy asked his mother about his missing sister, Rose Kennedy would only say that Rosemary had been sent away because she "could not keep up with" the other children.[2]

This was an unnerving thing to tell a child in a family where brothers and sisters were constantly pitted against each other in contests of strength and skill. Children who kept up won parental approval. Those who couldn't were sent to the kitchen to eat their dinner alone—or, as in Rosemary's case, banished from the clan.

In an Irish American family, there was no greater punishment than that. "[C]lan relationships—and Irish society was built upon the clans—were the binding cement that meant survival," wrote George Reedy in *From the Ward to the White House: The Irish in*

American Politics. "The most despised figure in all Irish literature is The Informer, the monster who betrays his fellow countrymen to the oppressor. There were no binding contracts enforceable in a court of law to hold together men and women scheming to circumvent power. That left only one instrument available for the enforcement of discipline—social ostracism. In a society organized along the lines of family ties, it was a potent instrument indeed. To be isolated from one's family was a one-way ticket to Hell."[3]

None of the Kennedy children felt this menace more keenly than Teddy, the youngest of nine. A sunny child with "a choirboy smile," Teddy seemed to lack the killer instinct of his older brothers. "Teddy bends over backwards to be fair when he's playing tennis," a friend once noted. "He's scrupulous about the calls, always giving the advantage to his opponent—and I haven't seen that in any other Kennedy."[4]

Though he was fat and awkward as a child, Ted tried to keep up with his brothers, especially with the eldest, Joe Jr., whom everyone in the family idolized. In 1944, Joe Jr.'s bomb-laden airplane exploded over the English coast, killing him instantly. Teddy was twelve years old at the time, and he retained a memory of two priests visiting his father at Hyannis Port to offer their comfort and consolation.

"Then [my father] came out of the sunporch," Teddy recalled, "and said, 'Children, your brother Joe has been lost. He died flying a volunteer mission. I want you to be particularly good to your Mother.' "[5]

Years later, after John Kennedy became president, he ruminated on how Ted's life had been influenced by Joe Jr.

"So if you say what was Joe's influence," JFK said, "it was pressure to do your best. Then the example that Joe and I had set put pressure on Bobby to do his best. The pressure of all the others on Teddy came to bear so that he had to do his best. It was a chain reaction started by Joe, that touched me, and all my brothers and sisters."[6]

The family tragedies didn't end there. In May 1948, while sixteen-year-old Ted was attending Milton Academy, south of Boston, he received word that his favorite sister, Kathleen, the widow of William John Robert Cavendish, the heir of the 10th duke of Devonshire, had died in another plane accident. And so Ted came of age at a time when three of his siblings were enshrined in the family pantheon as iconic figures. Rosemary was a martyr; Joe Jr., a hero; and Kathleen, a victim. It was hard enough to compete with your siblings as the youngest of nine; it was impossible to compete with the idealized memories of Rosemary, Joe Jr., and Kathleen. Surely Ted must have wondered why the last and the least had been spared while the best and the brightest had been cut off in the flower of youth.

"When you have older [children]," Rose Kennedy said, "they're the ones that seem more important. When the ninth comes along you have to make more of an effort to tell bedtime stories and be interested in swimming matches. There were seventeen years between my oldest and my youngest child and I had been telling bedtime stories for twenty years."[7]

If Teddy could claim any distinction at all, it was as the family clown. His nickname was "Fat Stuff,"[8] and, according to one family biographer, he was "so slow of foot that Bobby or even Jack could dance around him and run down the expanse of lawn for a touchdown."[9]

Not surprisingly, he was the target of merciless teasing, even by his own mother. "I think [Teddy] has put on ten pounds . . . ," his mother wrote in a round-robin letter to her children in 1942, when Ted was ten years old. "He dances very well, has remarkable rhythm, and shakes his head like a veteran when he does the conga. He only fell down once last week, so he is improving. . . ."[10]

Rose was still making fun of her son nearly twenty years later. "Jack gets a great kick out of seeing Ted dance," she wrote in November 1961, "as Ted has [a] great sense of rhythm but he is big & has such a big derrière it is funny to see him throw himself around. . . ."[11]

Many chroniclers of the Kennedy family have noted that Joe Kennedy was away from home for long stretches during the time his youngest son was growing up. One of Ted's classmates at Fessenden, a prep school in West Newton, Massachusetts, recalled that Joe and Rose Kennedy never once visited their son during his two years at the school.[12]

Rose was away a lot of the time, too; she took more than a dozen trips to Europe in the first five years of Teddy's life. However, in the absence of Teddy's father, Rose ruled (in person or through surrogates) with absolute authority. For instance, although Joe Kennedy boasted that he gave each of his children a thousand dollars for not smoking or drinking—and put them on the honor system—it was actually Rose who was the enforcer. "I got the idea from the Rockefellers," she said, "and I told Joe."[13] It was she, not their father, who meted out discipline and punishment.

JOSEPH PATRICK KENNEDY was one of those odd historic figures who are showered with tributes and honors during most of their lifetime and then heaped with abuse in their final years. Throughout the 1920s and '30s, while he was amassing one of the great American fortunes, he was hailed as a brilliant businessman and financier, a valued adviser to presidents, and, for a brief moment, a presidential contender himself. As ambassador to Great Britain during the years before World War II, he seriously misjudged Adolf Hitler's murderous intentions and became a leading advocate of appeasing Nazi Germany. But even then—after he had been rebuffed by President Franklin Roosevelt and recalled home—he continued to wield considerable political influence. The high-water mark of his career came late in life, when he was seventy-two years old and helped engineer the election of his son as president of the United States. For the next eleven months—from Inauguration Day in January 1961 until he suffered a major stroke on December 19 of that year—he was, after President John Kennedy, the second most powerful man in America.

Joe's sons grew up idolizing their father; they could not imagine him doing anything wrong. They came of age when he was still a revered figure in business and political circles, and although they eventually acknowledged some of his shortcomings, they never seriously challenged his preeminence or thought of him without deep affection.

Bobby and Ted were dismayed when Joe Kennedy's reputation came under sustained attack shortly after President Kennedy's assassination in 1963. Starting with Richard J. Whalen's 1964 *The Founding Father*, biographers found little to admire about Joe Kennedy. From then on, he was regularly portrayed as a ruthless crook, a stock swindler, and a bootlegger with ties to the Mob. It was said that he cared for his sons as a narcissist cares for others—as an extension of himself. He was the source of his sons' self-esteem, the one to whom they looked to validate their choices in everything from their life's work to their marriage partners. If he produced several outstanding offspring, he also set a deplorable example, encouraging his sons to treat women as disposable objects.

Ted did not recognize his father in this scathing portrait. Rather, he remembered his father as a benign but firm parent who displayed a sincere interest in his sons' welfare. His father made his presence felt with a steady stream of letters. These letters to his sons were full of messages of self-improvement and exhortations "to work on their handwriting, their grades, their attitudes, or their eating habits."[14]

"Dear Teddy," his father wrote to his eleven-year-old son on October 5, 1943, "I . . . got your report from school and boy: it is the worst one you ever had. In the fifth of your class you didn't pass in English or Geography and you only got 60 in Spelling and History. That is terrible—you can do better than that. You wouldn't want to have people say that Joe and Jack Kennedy's brother was such a bad student, so get on your toes."[15]

Again, on May 8, 1945, his father wrote: "Dear Teddy: I received your report for May fourth. You certainly fell down badly from the previous report and dropped to the 4th/fifth rather than the second. You can do better than this. Coming down to the last stages of the lap, a good runner doesn't quit at the finish—that's the time he puts on the speed! So get busy."[16]

And yet again, on January 31, 1946: "Dear Ted: I am sending $50 up to the school with instructions to let you have what you need. Your letters are coming through all right, but your penmanship hasn't improved much. You still spell 'no' know. Now, know means if you understand something, but if someone says, 'Are you going swimming?' and you say 'no' it is *no*—not know. Skating is not 'scating'; it is '*skating*,' and tomorrow you spell wrong. You spell it 'tommorow'; it is '*tomorrow*.' You spell slaughter as slauter. It is '*slaughter*.' You really ought to do a little more work on the writing and spelling. You are getting pretty old now [he was almost fourteen], and it looks rather babyish. . . . I am sorry to see that you are starving to death. I can't imagine that ever happening to you if there was anything at all to eat around, but then you can spare a few pounds. . . ."[17]

"The seeds of Ted Kennedy's problems in later life, and they were monumental, were planted in him by his father, who, quite literally, charted the lives and careers of his sons," wrote Dr. Thomas C. Reeves, reflecting the consensus opinion of historians. "Trying to adapt himself to Joe's standards, Teddy was thrust into a world he never wanted and couldn't handle. Raised by a father who drove him to compete and succeed, whatever the cost, Teddy was left in a moral vacuum."[18]

THE INFLUENCE OF Joseph and Rose Kennedy, for better or worse, on their youngest son has never been open to debate. But it begs an important question. For if Ted Kennedy was merely the creation of a ruthless father and a cold and callous mother, how did one explain Ted's exemplary behavior in the United States Senate? How could a man reared by such "bad" parents win such high praise from his colleagues for his warmth, thoughtfulness, and decency?

For a more nuanced understanding of Edward Kennedy, it might be helpful to recognize how *Ted* saw his father and mother, not only how *others* saw them. To Ted, his father was a man of "generosity, humor, and heart. . . . who was maligned . . . by those who never knew him and made no effort to find out." Whether this was an accurate assessment of Joe Kennedy, or whether it represented Ted's idealization of his father, was less important than the fact that Ted clung to this view all his life. He *perceived* his father as a man who was always ready to give more than was necessary, and this *perception* helped shape Ted's approach to public life.

As for his mother, Ted viewed her as a benevolent, warmhearted, and virtuous woman—not the heartless bullying old harridan portrayed in most of the hundreds of books that have been published about the Kennedy family.

"[O]nce he was grown, Rose began to favor Teddy," wrote Barbara Gibson, Rose Kennedy's personal secretary and close companion for many years. "He was the son most like her father. Tall and fat where John Fitzgerald was short and wiry, Ted nonetheless had the sense of humor her father enjoyed. He was like the stereotypical beloved, drunken Irish uncle who has ale in one hand and a tale of blarney coming from his lips.

"After the deaths of Joe junior, Jack, and Bob," Gibson continued, "Ted's importance grew. As Mrs. Kennedy would often say, had she not gone against the 'wisdom' of others and let herself get pregnant, she would have had no sons left at all.

"The relationship between mother and son was flirtatious. She always wanted him to see her as being special. The daughters Pat, Jean, and Eunice would come to lunch and were likely to encounter their mother in a dressing gown and pink pajamas on her way to take a nap. . . . But with Teddy she would not be dressed for the [nap]. . . . Instead she would put on one of her colorful suits from Courrèges, add a matching wide-brimmed hat, and modify her voice so it was girlish. They were more like close friends who knew how to make each other laugh than mother and son."[19]

On November 29, 1967, when Ted was thirty-five years old—a United States senator and a married man with three children—Rose sent him a note that would have been more appropriately addressed to a teenager: "Dear Teddy, Sometimes when I am speaking, people ask me about drinking and smoking. Did you ever get your money for not drinking and did you keep your pledge?"[20]

On November 4, 1968, Rose wrote: "Dear Teddy, Did you ever

think of eating an apple at noontime? I used to send apples to the boys at school. They are very good in New England this time of the year, and much more thinning than other desserts."[21]

On January 15, 1969: "Dear Teddy, I watched President Johnson last night on television and there were several shots of you. I suggest that you applaud all the time. If you do not, you appear indifferent and this is plainly captured on camera."[22]

May 18, 1969: "Dear Ted, I wish you would check the pronunciation of the word 'nuclear.' You pronounce it as though it were spelled 'nucular,' but I believe it should be pronounced 'nu-cle-ar.' "[23]

Alone among the Kennedy brothers, Ted remained extremely close to his mother all his adult life.

"Every morning [at Hyannis Port]," recalled Douglas Kennedy, the tenth child of Robert and Ethel Kennedy, "[Uncle Teddy] would structure his day around [his mother Rose]. He was constantly talking to her. Tell[ing] her the whole story of the day in a jolly, gregarious way . . . describing to her what happened. . . ."[24]

In an interview for this book, one of Ted's former girlfriends recalled how amazed she was to see the power that Rose still exercised over her youngest son. "In Rose's declining years, when she was senile," she said, "Ted went to her room every night that he was in Hyannis Port and spent sometimes hours behind a closed door talking to her, holding her hands, then, after she fell asleep, tiptoeing away.

"At one point," she continued, "Ted admitted to me that he had tried to win his mother's approval, but that he never felt he received the praise he so craved. It was, to him, the great failure of his life. It hurt him deeply. It's a pain he will definitely take to his grave."[25]

In the 1990s, shortly after the publication of Nigel Hamilton's scathing portrayal of Rose Kennedy in his best-selling biography *JFK: Reckless Youth*, the sixty-year-old senator—along with his sisters Jean Kennedy Smith, Eunice Kennedy Shriver, and Patricia Kennedy Lawford—issued a rare public defense of their mother. Prepared by the senator's staff, the letter was printed on the Op-Ed page of the *New York Times*. "The author's claim that Mother 'never kissed or touched and rarely saw' her children is ridiculous," the letter stated, adding that Rose was the "glue that held our family together."[26]

However, the senator and his sisters agreed with Nigel Hamilton on one essential point—namely, that Rose Kennedy was a far more important figure in her children's formative years than she was normally given credit for.

TED'S RELATIONSHIP WITH his parents was not an easy one. But then, Joe and Rose Kennedy were not easy, undemanding people. For all their money, they felt beset and assailed by a WASP establishment that looked down on Irish Catholics. Both Joe and Rose harbored a deep resentment of the high and mighty, and urged their sons to go into public life in order to even the score. "To those whom much is given, much is expected," Ted's mother used to say. It was one of the great paradoxes of Ted's life that his millionaire parents taught him to identify with the underdog.

Ted Kennedy's idealism has been much commented upon by sympathetic journalists. For instance, the late columnist Jack Newfield traced the senator's liberal politics, which were far more left-leaning than those of his brother Jack, to Ted's tragic sense of life. "He identifies with hurt and loss," Newfield wrote. "And he is able to translate his empathy into public remedies and reforms."[27]

For most of his life, until he married Victoria Reggie in 1992, Ted Kennedy's behavior oscillated between the constructive law-maker and the destructive libertine, the devoted father and the shamelessly unfaithful husband. Naturally, no single psychological explanation could ever account for this ever-changing, kaleidoscopic behavior.

However, there was one factor that brought everything into focus: Ted's particular form of alcoholism. There are many kinds of alcoholics—from falling-down drunks to recovering alcoholics who white-knuckle their way through sobriety. Ted Kennedy fell into the category of binge drinker—someone who could go for days, even sometimes for weeks, without alcohol but who, once he took a drink, was instantly out of control and could not stop drinking. When he was sober, Ted was a person of integrity and honor. Drunk, he became someone else. Alcohol made him reckless; it unleashed his destructive demons.

3

A︎FTER LUNCH AT Union Station—"the only place in town serving genuine New England clam chowder and oyster stew," according to Jack Kennedy[1]—the new senator offered to show his brother around the Senate. They climbed into a wicker coach on the Senate monorail and headed toward the chamber.

Despite its broad, gleaming halls, heroic statuary, and grandiose architecture, the Senate was an intimate institution. It venerated custom and tradition and had not changed much in the past several decades. Most of its members lived full-time in Washington or its suburbs and returned to their home states only for holidays, vacations, and reelection campaigns. No one, except the majority and minority leaders of the two parties, had large staffs. That meant each member had to do a lot of his own research and spend a good deal of time with his fellow senators. As a result, senators got to know each other well, which helped them become effective deal cutters. Unlike the institution of the presidency, where one man made decisions, the Senate required coalition building in order to get things done.

The Kennedy brothers arrived at the dimly lit Senate chamber. Television lights had not yet been introduced. In the fading afternoon light, Jack pointed out several senators, including Everett Dirksen, the conservative Republican from Illinois, who was napping at his desk.

The Senate, Jack told Ted, was still ruled by members of The Club, mostly Southern Democrats and conservative Republicans, who were bound by their common distaste for Negro civil rights, government regulation, and social change.[2] Young members were expected to defer to their elders, to seek their counsel, and to go along to get along. The virtues most admired were the three "C's"—courtesy, congeniality, and cooperation.

Each day after the Senate adjourned, its members put aside their political differences and renewed their personal friendships. James Eastland, the rabid segregationist from Mississippi, would sit down and have a few drinks with Paul Douglas, the ultraliberal Democrat from Illinois. Alcohol greased the political skids, and there was a lot of hard drinking and womanizing. Even senators with the most unblemished reputations, such as Tennessee's crusading, crime-busting Estes Kefauver, carried on extramarital affairs.

In the Kennedy household, alcohol—the scourge of the Irish—had been discouraged; Joe Kennedy rationed his guests to one drink before dinner.[3] Jack and Bobby drank moderately. But Ted was a budding alcoholic, and like most alcoholics, he felt comfortable around other heavy drinkers. It may not have been lost on him that the boozy Senate men's club provided an ideal setting for someone who enjoyed drinking to excess without the guilt that usually went along with it.

But alcohol, though important, was by no means the only thing that attracted Ted to the Senate. As the youngest child in a big family, he had grown up learning to pay respect to his father and brothers, and for the rest of his life he instinctively deferred to his seniors. He never tried to triumph over his brothers, easily accepting his place in a hierarchy. And since he did not share his brother Jack's irresistible compulsion to become president, the Senate seemed a far more appealing home to him than it did to Jack.

And so, after his brother's tour, Ted applied for a summer internship in the Senate. "I talked with him," said Carl Marcy, an aide on the Senate Foreign Relations Committee, "and explained we didn't take interns at that time because by the time they were properly cleared and knew their way around, the summer was over. . . . The fellow was very polite, and stood up to leave. And his name was Kennedy. On the way out I said, 'Are you by any chance related to Jack Kennedy—Senator Kennedy on the committee?' He said, 'Yes, I'm his brother Teddy.' So he turned and left. No, he hadn't mentioned it till I asked."

"Yes, that's the way it happened," Ted said later, "and that's the last time I ever applied for a job without using my brother's name!"[4]

Ted had been away from Harvard for nearly two and a half years, and upon his readmission in the fall of 1953, he began to drink more heavily and display signs of a dangerous self-destructive streak. It was hard to explain the eruption of this negative behavior. Perhaps, after his stint as a military policeman, he bridled at the constraints of being an underclassman. Or perhaps he thought that having a famous father and brother entitled him to do whatever he pleased. Whatever the cause, the most affable of Joe Kennedy's sons revealed a newly aggressive side to his personality.

He was ejected by a referee from a rugby match after getting into three fistfights with opposing players. "I've thought a lot about that game since," the referee said. "Rugby is a character-building sport. Players learn how to conduct themselves on the field with the idea that they will learn how to conduct themselves in life. Knocks are given and taken, but you must play by the rules. When a player loses control of himself three times in a single afternoon, to my mind that is a sign that, in a crisis, the man is not capable of thinking clearly and acting rationally. Such a man will panic under pressure."[5]

Ted displayed another outburst of temper during a sailing vacation off the coast of Maine. While rowing a dinghy ashore, he and a friend were heckled by a passenger aboard a large yacht. According to his friend, Ted "spun the dinghy around so fast I almost fell out of it. The next thing I knew, he was on the yacht and the man was being thrown overboard and all the women were screaming and running below to hide in their cabins. . . . In no time, all of the men—there were about eight of them—were in the water. I never saw anything like it."[6]

One of his early biographers, James MacGregor Burns, referred to Ted's "volcanic physical energy"—a trait fueled by his Brobdingnagian consumption of alcohol. Ted, said his Harvard roommate John Varick Tunney, son of the famous heavyweight-boxing champion, "turns into quite a different person when he isn't working."[7]

After Harvard, Ted was admitted to the University of Virginia Law School, where his drunken exploits in his broken-down convertible earned him the nickname "Cadillac Eddie." On one occasion, a deputy sheriff pursued Ted in a high-speed car chase—lights flashing, sirens roaring—that ended in a suburban driveway, with

Ted cowering on the floor under the steering wheel. He was cited for so many traffic violations while at the University of Virginia that his brother Bobby said: "My mother wants to know on what side of the court my brother is going to appear when he gets out of law school, attorney or defendant."[8]

4

J OE THOUGHT THE children would never get married because they all enjoyed going out together so much," Rose Kennedy once said.[1]

To ward off such a possibility, Joe had personally picked out wives for Bobby and Jack—the wealthy Ethel Skakel for Bobby, the socially prominent Jacqueline Bouvier for Jack. Now all of his children, except the hapless Rosemary and Ted, were married. But Joe already had his eye on a suitable Catholic girl for his youngest son. She was Jackie's stepsister, Nina Auchincloss, an attractive young woman with an upper-class accent who, like Jackie, had her heart set on becoming a journalist. However, Nina had other ideas. She ended up marrying a rich Republican instead of a rich Kennedy Democrat.[2]

And so, it fell to Ted's shy, reserved sister, Jean Kennedy Smith, the second youngest of Joe and Rose's nine children, to act as matchmaker. In the fall of 1957, at the start of his second year in law school, twenty-five-year-old Ted Kennedy traveled to Purchase, New York, to help dedicate the new Kennedy Physical Education Building at Manhattanville College, an all-girls Catholic school. As Ted rose to speak, four Kennedy women who had attended Manhattanville were in the audience—his mother, his sisters Jean and Eunice, and his sister-in-law Ethel.

Joe Kennedy had donated a great deal of money for the building in memory of one of its most famous alumnae, his daughter Kathleen, and the Manhattanville nuns had made it abundantly clear that all seniors were required to attend the event. However, one of the seniors, twenty-one-year-old Joan Bennett, had chosen to skip the ceremony because she thought it would be just "another boring event . . . with the nuns."[3] Suddenly, her roommate, Margot Murray, burst into the room, where Joan was working on a term paper, and declared breathlessly that Joan was in trouble. Her absence had been noticed by the nuns, which would automatically result in demerits.[4]

"Maybe if you come down real fast," Margot suggested, "the student government girl who gives out the demerits will see you and assume you've been there through the whole ceremony."

"So," Joan recalled, "I got out of my old bathrobe, jumped into something appropriate, and ran over. The next thing I knew I was standing with Margot, and Jean Smith, Ted's sister, came up to me and said, 'Aren't you Joan Bennett? Remember we met last August?'

"Well, when she spotted me at this reception and came over to talk to me, I didn't know Jean Smith was one of the Kennedys. I had never even heard of the Kennedys! I just took no interest in current events; my lowest grade in college was in current events. Jean said she'd like me to meet her little brother or her younger brother, and I'd almost expected to meet someone knee-high. . . ."[5]

. . .

JOAN BENNETT WAS a five-foot-eight-inch blonde who did not need any makeup to enhance her natural beauty. She was named after her mother, Virginia Joan Bennett, but her parents called her Joan so as not to have two Ginnys in the house.[6] Coming of age in the prosperous 1950s, Joan appeared to lead a charmed life. Her father was a successful advertising executive and an avid amateur actor who took his two girls, Joan and her younger sister, Candace, to practically every musical that opened on Broadway.[7] Her mother was a stay-at-home mom. Her sister, Candy, was a popular high-school cheerleader who helped Joan master the piano. The family belonged to the Siwanoy Country Club and had a summer home in Alstead, New Hampshire.[8] And their major residence—a pink-and-gray four-bedroom house in Bronxville, an affluent suburb of New York City—was filled with sunshine and music.

And yet, her close friends would remember Joan as a young woman riddled with self-doubt. For instance, she had perfect pitch and loved to receive praise for her performances on the piano, but she suffered from stage fright and did not enjoy giving recitals.[9] She was self-conscious about her looks, but she forced herself to show up at auditions for TV commercials, and she became the Revlon Hairspray girl for a while on *The $64,000 Question*. She adored her mother, but she was secretly ashamed that Ginny (as she called her) was an alcoholic.[10] She had many boyfriends, but none of them ever lived up to her idealized image of her father, who was also an alcoholic.

"When Joan talked about her father," wrote Marcia Chellis, who in later years was her administrative assistant and biographer, "he reminded me in some ways of the man [Ted Kennedy] she would eventually marry. Harry Bennett was tall, handsome, charming, an actor in neighborhood theatrical productions. Joan described herself as a compliant, sweet, shy little girl who obediently accomplished all that was expected of her. . . . To me it seemed that she had tried very hard to please her father, as she would later try so hard to please her husband."[11] (In this regard, Joan resembled another Kennedy wife—Jacqueline Bouvier.)

When Joan was seventeen years old—just as her braces came off, her figure filled out, and boys started taking notice—her father (whom she called Harry, not Dad) took her with him on a business trip to Florida.[12]

"I was working like crazy," Harry Bennett said. "Ten, twelve, fourteen hours a day. I knew that I didn't give my family enough attention, but I was so busy earning a living. I missed having time with my family, and I thought it might be fun to take my little girl [Joan] away with me and have her all to myself, just for a week.

"I decided from the moment we left the front door of our house she would no longer be my daughter, but my date," he continued. "And I wooed her all that week, and took her out, not as my daughter, but as my sweetheart, if you want to call it that.

"Joan stayed up all night with me at nightclubs for the first time in her life, and we drank champagne together for the first time. We saw everything there was to be seen in Saint Petersburg, Tampa, and Gainesville. We went fishing, we went swimming, we did everything.

"She had the time of her life. And when we were on the plane coming home, she looked at me and said, 'I never knew adults could be so much fun.' "[13]

SHORTLY AFTER TED met Joan on the Manhattanville campus, he called her for a date.

"I had to be chaperoned everywhere," Joan remembered. "Nobody slept together. Nobody spent time alone. You were always in groups—at least if you were a Manhattanville girl."[14]

One time, she and Ted went skiing in Stowe, Vermont, with Margot Murray, Joan's roommate, and Margot's boyfriend, who had gone to Harvard with Ted. Another time, Joan invited Ted to the Bennetts' summer home in New Hampshire, where they went to a square dance and, she recalled, Ted "gave me a glimpse of how much fun he was. . . . Ted Kennedy was up there doing the calling. . . . Everybody loved him."[15]

During that same visit, Joan's mother bought paints, canvases, and easels for her guests and sent them out to paint the view from the top of a nearby mountain.

"I remember Ted Kennedy painting the best paintings of anybody there," Joan said. "There was a contest and he won."[16]

In the summer of 1958, Ted invited Joan to Hyannis Port to meet his family. By then, Rose Kennedy had done a background check on Joan with Mother Elizabeth O'Byrne, the president of Manhattanville College, who had nothing but good things to say about Joan and her family.

"I spent a whole week with Rose and Ted," Joan said. "I remember we played the piano together a lot. I remember walking on the beach with Ted a lot. Ted would play eighteen holes. It was very cozy, I thought."[17]

That Ted was less than enthusiastic about getting married was a gross understatement. He did not want to give up his life of sexual adventurism—the only area of his life that was not under his mother and father's control. However, his father made it clear that Ted was expected to get married. Dutiful son that he was, Ted waited until the next time he and Joan were alone on the beach, then turned to her and said:

"What do you think about getting married?"

"Well," Joan replied to this not-quite-lavish offer of marriage, "I guess it's not such a bad idea."

"What do we do next?" Ted asked.[18]

The next thing was for Joan to meet Ted's father, who had just arrived home from his annual summer vacation in the south of France.[19] Laurence Leamer, author of *The Kennedy Men*, has given us one version of that meeting.

"The sixty-nine-year-old patriarch sat in his great wing chair in the far end of the living room, looking at Joan like a monarch holding court," Leamer wrote. "Joan walked tentatively into the room and sat at Joe's feet on an ottoman. 'Do you love my son?' Joe asked. It was the crucial question, but it was rarely asked so boldly. This was no social chitchat but an intense interview. Joe had been home only a few hours, but he seemed to know everything about Joan and her family. . . ."[20]

The scene rang true, except for one thing: Joan disputed the accuracy of Leamer's account. In an interview with the *New York Times'* Adam Clymer, Joan cast her meeting with Joe Kennedy in far more positive terms. Joe "was a charmer," she said, and she had not felt the least bit intimidated by his blunt "Do you love my son?" question. It wasn't asked in a stern way. "Right from the beginning," said Joan, "I didn't think he was a scary guy."[21]

In fact, Joe Kennedy turned out to be a vitally important surrogate suitor in Ted's courtship of Joan. Joe wooed Joan on Ted's behalf just as he had wooed Jackie for Jack. It would be no exaggeration to say that Joan agreed to marry Ted at least in part because of Joe. He, rather than Ted, made her feel wanted.

But despite Joe's intervention, there was still a major obstacle to a wedding—namely, Ted's reservations about getting married. "I was young and naive then," Joan said, "but looking back, there were warning signals. We didn't see each other from the time of [Ted's] proposal until the engagement party."[22]

Ted was late for his own engagement party, which was held at the Bennetts' home in Bronxville. "So he wouldn't embarrass my mother, he chose to come in the back way, through the maid's quarters," Joan said.[23] Ted had not even bothered to buy an engagement ring; he had left that task to his father, who sent a huge emerald-cut diamond engagement ring over to Harry Bennett's office.[24] Harry slipped the unopened ring box into Ted's hand at the appropriate moment.

That night, when their engagement became official, Joan was still a virgin. "The only reason he wanted to marry me," Joan said years later, "was because he couldn't get me any other way."[25]

HOWEVER, IT WAS Joan, not Ted, who got cold feet at the last moment. She went to her father and pleaded with him to postpone the wedding. But when Harry Bennett traveled to Hyannis Port and raised the subject of a postponement with Ted and Joe Kennedy, Joe blew his stack.

"He said they're not going to put in the papers that my son is being tossed over," according to Mary Lou McCarthy, Joe's niece. "He forced the issue. He was God. The wedding was going to happen whether Ted or Joan liked it or not. I told Joan, 'You can't cure the addicted woman chaser.' And she said, 'I have no choice but to try, do I? What else can I do?' From the beginning, she was in trouble, and she seemed to know [it]."[26]

The wedding was held on a frigid day in November 1958, at St. Joseph's Roman Catholic Church in Bronxville. At Joe Kennedy's insistence, his friend Francis Cardinal Spellman, the spiritual leader of the New York archdiocese, officiated at the ceremony. As a wedding gift, a friend hired a photographer to film the wedding, and Joan's ad-man father had microphones placed around the altar.

"Later," said Joan, "when Ted told Jack about the 'bug,' Jack was really embarrassed because when they were behind the altar, he was giving Ted a big-brother-to-little-brother talk about marriage!"[27] Jack's advice, Joan noted, consisted of assuring Ted that, wedding vows or no wedding vows, Ted could continue to sleep with as many women as he pleased.[28]

After a brief honeymoon, Joan moved into Ted's rented off-campus house in Charlottesville, where he had one more year at the University of Virginia Law School. "I do remember," said Joan, "that when I moved into the house, Ted dismissed the maid! I had to clean, cook, do the laundry, and I really learned a lot. It was fun—for a while!"[29]

When it came time for Ted to cram for the bar exam, he told Joan that he did not want her around. "He said I would be a distraction," Joan recalled.[30] Joe Kennedy offered to take Joan off his son's hands; he invited her to go with him to his favorite getaway, the Hôtel du Cap Eden-Roc in the south of France.

Given Joe Kennedy's well-known penchant for making passes at his son's girlfriends, Joan might well have had some reservations about traveling with him to Europe. But if she did, she didn't express them to anyone. Of her time alone with Joe at the Hôtel du Cap Eden-Roc, Joan had little to say.

"We would sit out under the stars," she recalled, "and listen to the BBC concerts."[31]

5

——

During JOHN KENNEDY'S campaign for the White House in 1959 and 1960, he assigned Ted, who was fresh out of law school, to manage his operations in eleven western states plus Alaska and Hawaii. It was a huge expanse of territory and a daunting political task, since most of the states Ted was responsible for were rock-solid Republican. "All they gave me was a two-page memorandum with about ten different names on it, plus a speech my brother made in Montana in 1957," Ted recalled. "The rest was up to me. Lucky I learned how to fly a plane when I went to law school."[1]

Ted and Joan moved to San Francisco with their infant daughter, Kara, who was born on February 27, 1960.[2] After Joan recovered from giving birth, the couple traveled together on the campaign trail, but it soon became apparent that by splitting up they could draw twice the audience and become twice as effective.[3]

When Ted showed up at a ski-jump contest in Wisconsin, he

asked for permission to address the crowd of ten thousand people. One of the officials, displaying a bizarre sense of humor, agreed that Ted could use the public-address system, but only if he made the hundred-and-eighty-foot Olympic ski jump himself. "I wanted to get off the jump, take off my skis, or even go down the side," Ted said. "But if I did, I was afraid my brother would hear of it. And if he heard of it, I knew I would be back in Washington licking stamps and addressing envelopes for the rest of the campaign."[4]

While Ted barely survived such challenges, Joan was involved in her own risky adventures. "I remember going down into a coal mine with Jack," she said. "I'm from Bronxville. This is like another world. At the coal mines, they were very sweet about it, but they whistled. I had very good legs and lots of blonde hair. . . . I got more attention than [Jack] did."[5]

That didn't sit well with the candidate, who was less than thrilled about being upstaged by his sister-in-law. Jack issued orders that Joan was to be barred from all blue-collar events; she could appear at women's teas. (After the election, JFK presented his family and staff with engraved silver cigarette cases. Joan's was inscribed "To Joan Kennedy/Too Beautiful to Use."[6])

In the course of their travels, Ted and Joan talked about moving to Arizona after the election. Above all, Ted wanted to put some distance between himself and his overbearing father. "His main reason," said Joan, "was that in a new state, among new people, he would have to succeed or fail on his own."[7] But shortly after Jack won the election, Joe Kennedy summoned Ted and Joan to a meeting. "Jack is president," he said. "Bob is going to be attorney general. Teddy and Joansie, it's your turn. Get your fat asses up to Boston. You are going to run for the Senate."

. . .

· · ·

TED TRIED TO argue with his father. To begin with, he said, he had no interest in running for the Senate seat Jack had just vacated. Ted was approaching his twenty-ninth birthday, which meant he was still a year shy of being eligible to occupy a seat in the Senate. What's more, he did not feel qualified for such high office.[8] But Joe Kennedy brushed aside his son's misgivings and expressed contempt for his scruples. "Look," he said, "I paid for it [the Senate seat from Massachusetts]. It belongs to the family."[9]

The brief clash of wills between father and son represented one of several important turning points in Ted's life, for it would be the last time he ever attempted to overrule his father and assert his independence. He and Joan gave up their dream of moving to Arizona. Instead, Ted went to Africa with a group of U.S. senators to gain some foreign-policy experience and to add a bit of gravitas to his featherlight résumé.

"In the meantime," said Joan, "I'm sent up to Boston [to] rent a place." While the new apartment was being decorated, Ted, Joan, and Kara lived in an unheated, dingy loft. "It was a garret," Joan said. "We felt like we were part of *La Bohème*."[10]

Ted's likely opponent in the Democratic primary was Massachusetts attorney general Edward McCormack, a well-respected prosecutor and nephew of the Speaker of the House of Representatives. "Gee, I don't want to run against Eddie," Ted told Thomas "Tip" O'Neill, a congressman from the 11th District, which Jack had once represented in the House. "You know, it's not good for the party, it's not good for the relationships in Washington. . . . I'll pay—we understand Eddie owes a hundred thousand dollars. We'll take care of his expenses. . . . Anything that he's interested in . . . he can have. . . . My brother can make him an ambassador."[11]

When McCormack spurned Ted's proposal (which also included a lucrative offer to become the lawyer for several Kennedy family business enterprises), the Kennedys took off the gloves. "With Robert Kennedy's approval, Justice Department records were searched for anything detrimental about McCormack," wrote Ralph G. Martin, "and there was a similar search in the Pentagon files for anything useful in McCormack's service record."[12]

If Joe Kennedy could not bribe or intimidate McCormack, he was determined to outspend him. Ted was given an unlimited campaign budget, and he hired six private secretaries, two part-time office assistants, and delegates to represent him with all twenty-six nationalities and ethnic groups in the Boston area.[13] Joe persuaded his son-in-law Steve Smith, who had run Jack's successful presidential campaign, to get back in harness and run Ted's campaign. Within a few weeks, Smith had two hundred and forty workers on Ted's campaign payroll.

"Teddy and his brothers considered a political campaign an athletic competition by another name," said speechwriter Milton Gwirtzman. "Teddy wanted to get in as many campaign stops as possible, just as he wanted to get in as many downhill ski runs, to get in that nineteenth run even though it was getting dark and sometimes dangerous. . . . Teddy got down to an absolute minimum the time it took to get up in the morning, shower, shave, get dressed, and be ready to go out campaigning. He got it down to five minutes so he could be down on the wharf at six thirty in the morning shaking hands with fishermen."[14]

Joan was pregnant during the early stages of the political race; she gave birth to her second child, Edward M. Kennedy Jr., on September 26, 1961. By late that year, she was ready to join Ted on the campaign trail.

"Saddle up, Joansie!" Ted would tell his wife. "We've got a ten o'clock tea at Lowell, then another one at four. There's a banquet tonight in Boston, and after that a coffee in Lawrence. We should be back [home] tonight. Did I tell you six are coming for lunch tomorrow? Could you get lobster?"[15]

"It was so much fun," Joan recalled. "It was just a bunch of us kids. Those were the good years of our marriage. . . . It was so wonderful to feel like I was important and needed and wanted, and all those wonderful words that never quite happened again."[16]

THE FORMAL ANNOUNCEMENT of Ted's candidacy, on March 14, 1962, was greeted by hoots of derision from the press and the political establishment. He was widely viewed as a lightweight who was riding on the president's coattails. James Reston, the *New York Times*' respected Washington bureau chief, wrote: "One Kennedy is a triumph, two Kennedys at the same time is a miracle, but three could easily be regarded by many voters as an invasion." "Before you know it," declared an editorial in the *Chicago Tribune*, "we are in 1964 with Caroline coming up fast and John F. Jr. just behind her." Not to be outdone, the *Washington Post*'s editorialists described Ted as a modest man "with much to be modest about."[17]

According to rumors that were making the rounds, Ted also had much to hide, especially the cheating episode that got him kicked out of Harvard. "I had [the story]," said Robert L. Healy, Washington bureau chief of the *Boston Globe*, "but there was a stumbling block. Harvard had a firm policy of not revealing any of its records. In today's world of journalistic leaks, the story would have been printed immediately, but back then we required documentation before publishing. I had to get the okay or forget about it. I asked the White House to open the Harvard record and was summoned down to the Oval Office. I had three meetings there with the president. . . . Jack was pretty shrewd. He would have liked the story included in some kind of profile of Ted, which would have buried it, and I said 'no soap.' "[18]

Eventually, however, the editors of the *Globe* agreed to a compromise. They ran a story with a headline—TED KENNEDY TELLS ABOUT HARVARD EXAMINATION INCIDENT—that did not mention the word "cheating." And as far as the "incident" in the headline was concerned, that was not described until the fifth paragraph. Years later, Healy explained to the *New York Times*' Adam Clymer that the publisher of the *Globe* had softened the story because he "believed in not hurting the presidency."[19]

In the first of two debates between Ted and his Democratic primary opponent, McCormack got off the best line of the campaign: "If his name was Edward Moore, with his qualifications, with your qualifications, Teddy, your candidacy would be a joke, but nobody's laughing because his name is not Edward Moore. It's Edward Moore Kennedy."

After the debate, Milton Gwirtzman took a call from the president, who was eager to hear how his brother had performed. "On points, McCormack probably won," said Gwirtzman. "He made a lot of the people take the things he said about Ted and think about them, and he might have made some points. But on impression, on the general impression people get on television, Ted won, he was the good guy." To which the president replied, "None of this on the one hand, on the other hand! He's the candidate. He has to get up in the morning and go out and campaign. Tell him that he did great. None of this objective shit, not with somebody who's running."[20]

In the end, McCormack's harsh attacks backfired, creating more sympathy for Ted Kennedy than disapproval. As a result, Mc-Cormack lost the Democratic primary to Ted, who then went on to win the general election on November 6, 1962, by a landslide. But the architect of Ted's victory, his father, could not savor the triumph; three months before the launch of the campaign, seventy-three-year-old Joe Kennedy had suffered a stroke, and lost the power of speech.

WHEN EDWARD MOORE KENNEDY was sworn in as a United States senator, he joined one of democracy's oldest—and oddest—deliberative bodies. In the Senate, any piece of legislation that really matters is subject to a filibuster, which allows the minority to thwart the will of the majority. As a result, a senator frequently needs to round up a *supermajority* of sixty votes—the number required to invoke Rule 22, or cloture, in order to set a time limit on debate and clear the way for a vote.

The cloture rule places a premium on a certain kind of personality. You can't be an effective senator without being a compromiser, a coalition-builder, and one of the boys. From day one, it was clear that Ted Kennedy had all these talents in spades, and that he therefore had the makings of a great senator.

In the eyes of his fellow senators, Ted was an amiable, warmhearted, unassuming fellow with a great sense of humor. "Robust humor is both salient in Kennedy's character and a secret to his political success," noted the *Washington Post*'s Rick Atkinson. "He is a gifted mimic, whether imitating Italian ward heelers in New England [or] his grandfather's singsong Boston brogue. . . . He often lampoons himself, particularly his girth. . . . His puckish streak plays well on the Hill, where humor can heal even the most jagged political wounds. Two years ago, Kennedy and Sen. Strom Thurmond (R-S.C.) fell into a heated Labor Committee argument. . . . But as the two senators left the room for a meeting of the Judiciary Committee, Kennedy threw an arm around his colleague's shoulder. 'C'mon, Strom,' he urged, 'let's go upstairs and I'll give you a few judges.' "[21]

As the youngest of nine children, Ted found it natural to defer to his elders, an essential trait in a legislative body built on the foundation of seniority. In his early days, he fell under the spell of Michigan's charismatic liberal senator, Philip Aloysius Hart, who was nicknamed "the Conscience of the Senate."

"You can accomplish anything in Washington if you give others the credit," Phil Hart wisely counseled Ted. It was a piece of advice that Ted would follow for the rest of his career.

Another significant figure in the young senator's life was Walter Reuther, the head of the United Auto Workers. Reuther was a champion of a national health-care insurance system, and he used his considerable influence among Democrats on Capitol Hill to secure a seat for Ted on a health subcommittee. There, Ted launched what would become a half-century crusade for a national health-care bill.

Ted shared Reuther's political philosophy. "There is no greater calling than to serve your fellow men," Reuther was fond of saying. "There is no greater contribution than to help the weak. There is no greater satisfaction than to have done it well."[22]

Ted's deference to his elders and gracious self-effacement was all the more impressive because of his personal pipeline to the ultimate source of power in Washington—his brother, the president. When the handsome thirty-year-old freshman senator from Massachusetts stood on the floor of the Senate, he didn't have to utter a word; he just naturally emanated the aura of political power.

6

ALMOST SINGLEHANDEDLY, Joseph Kennedy had created a new phenomenon in American politics: the Kennedy Dynasty. He had put a son in the White House, another in the Justice Department, and a third in the United States Senate. It was widely assumed that after Jack's two terms, Bobby and Ted would follow him into the Oval Office. Together, the three brothers would rule for nearly a quarter of a century: Jack, 1961–1969; Bobby, 1969–1977; and Ted, 1977–1985.

But like so many best-laid plans in politics, this one never came to fruition. Exactly one year and sixteen days after Ted's victory, Jack was dead, and Joe Kennedy had to watch helplessly from his wheelchair as the Kennedy Dynasty crashed head-on into the Kennedy Curse.

· · ·

. . .

THE CRASH OCCURRED on Ted and Joan's fifth wedding anniversary. Washington's best caterers were setting up tables and centerpieces for a party planned for that night at the Kennedys' townhouse in Georgetown. Joan was at the Elizabeth Arden salon on Connecticut Avenue, getting her nails done and her hair lightened. Ted was at the Capitol, sitting in for the president pro tempore of the Senate. The chamber was practically empty; a half dozen members were lolling behind their desks, listening to Stuart Symington, the white-thatched Democrat from Missouri, drone on about the country's dire balance-of-payments situation.

It was Friday, November 22, 1963.

All of a sudden there was a commotion at the door, and William Langham Riedel, the Senate's press liaison officer, burst into the chamber and came running down the aisle and up to the rostrum. "Senator Kennedy," he said breathlessly, "Senator Kennedy, your brother the president has been shot!"[1]

Symington caught the panicky tone in Riedel's voice and stopped speaking in midsentence. He looked up at Ted. As Symington later recalled, Ted "sat back suddenly in his chair as if he had been hit by a whiplash. With typical Kennedy guts, he very slowly assembled his papers, picked them up, and walked out."[2]

HE'S DEAD," BOBBY said when Ted reached him on the phone at the White House. "You better call [our] mother and sisters."[3]

Ted and his sister Eunice hopped on a presidential helicopter and flew to Hyannis Port. There, they found Rose Kennedy walking alone on the beach. "Even when I heard Jack was shot," she said, "I thought, those things happen. I never thought the first moment that it was going to be serious. I never think the worst."[4] Joe Kennedy's private secretary, Diane Winter D'Alemberta, recalled: "The thing which ultimately brought me to grips with the incomprehensible reality was a hand-clapped cadence and the dear, familiar voice [of Rose Kennedy] repeating over and over again, 'No-crying-in-this-house! No-crying-in-this-house!' "[5]

Ted and Eunice went upstairs to break the news to their paralyzed father. Before Ted opened the door to his father's bedroom, he stationed Joe's private physician in the hallway outside, ready if necessary to administer a sedative. Then, with tears streaming down his cheeks, Ted told his father that Jack had been assassinated.

"Ted dropped to his knees and buried his face in his hands," nurse Rita Dallas said.[6]

"He's dead, Daddy, he's dead," Eunice cried.[7]

AFTER THE FUNERAL, someone asked Ted: "Is it ever going to end for you people?" To which he replied: "There are still more of us than there is trouble."[8]

That was a brave thing to say. But it was not true. His father was without the power of speech. His mother had become a religious zealot with a waning interest in worldly matters. Of Joe and Rose's nine children, three (Joe Jr., Kathleen, and Jack) were dead; a fourth (Rosemary) had been lobotomized into a vegetable-like existence; and a fifth (Patricia) was struggling with alcoholism. With each new blow to his family, Ted was stripped of one more source of emotional support.

Of course, there was still Bobby. But Bobby could not replace Jack as Ted's guide and counselor. Bobby might have been the brother closest to Ted in age, the one who spent the most time with Ted as he was growing up, but Jack had been Ted's guiding light. He, not

Bobby, represented everything Ted hoped to become—witty, stylish, charming, charismatic, and tough. Ted and Jack enjoyed the same Irish sense of humor, with its merciless needling and ragging. Jack was .dashing and a man of large appetites—traits that Ted particularly admired. Bobby was not cut from the same cloth.

"I miss him every time I see his children," Ted said of his assassinated brother. "I miss him every time I see the places, like Cape Cod, which had such meaning for him and still have for all of us. I miss him at the times our family used to get together, such as his birthday and Thanksgiving. I miss the chance to tell him about things I've done which I feel proud of, and I miss his encouragement and advice at times of difficulty. I miss him as you'd miss your best friend. . . ."[9]

And yet, it was one of the great ironies of Ted's life that he, as well as Bobby, missed a brother who was, in many respects, a glorified version of the flesh-and-blood Jack.

"After his death," wrote James Piereson, president of the conservative William E. Simon Foundation, "Kennedy was soon portrayed by family loyalists as something of a liberal hero who (had he lived) might have led the nation into a new age of peace, justice, and understanding. . . . This portrayal was encouraged by tributes and memorials inspired by Jacqueline Kennedy and friends and other family members of the slain president, and by numerous books published after the assassination, particularly those by presidential aides Arthur Schlesinger Jr. and Theodore Sorensen, both of whom portrayed the fallen president as the brightest star of the time and a leader impossible to replace."

Piereson continued: "Sorensen wrote that Kennedy was the equal of any of our earlier presidents. Schlesinger went further to say that 'He re-established the republic as the first generation of our founders saw it—young, brave, civilized, rational, gay, tough, questing, exultant in the excitement and potentiality of history.' There was a sense in these tributes that the loss of John F. Kennedy had deprived that nation and the world of a new beginning."[10]

Like Bobby, Ted embraced this romantic ideal, even though the legend did not fit the facts. From the time Jack entered politics in 1947 until the day he was shot sixteen years later, he steered a pragmatic and moderate course. He was an ardent Cold Warrior who approved assassination plots and increased the federal defense budget by billions of dollars. He was a fiscal conservative who cut taxes to stimulate the economy. His approach to civil rights and other liberal causes was governed by realism and caution. He even refused to pose for pictures with the Reverend Martin Luther King Jr. for fear that such photographs could cost him reelection.[11] He was, to use his own words, "a liberal without illusions."

But this was not the JFK whom Bobby and Ted chose to enshrine in memory. The legend, not the man, served as their template for Kennedy-style liberalism. Where the real JFK was careful never to get too far out in front of public opinion, Bobby and Ted embraced the mythic JFK who was lionized as a revolutionary cultural figure. Where the real JFK believed in arming for peace, Bobby and Ted rejected militant anticommunism and American exceptionalism (the idea that America is favored by Providence) as key elements of foreign policy.[12]

"President Kennedy," Bobby declared, "was more than just president of a country. He was the leader of young people everywhere. What he was trying to do was fight against hunger, disease, and poverty around the world. You and I as young people have a special responsibility to carry on the fight."[13]

What's more, Bobby and Ted accepted the fable that their brother was a martyr to a great cause. In their version of events, Jack, like Abraham Lincoln, was the champion of black America. Jack's role as a great emancipator had made him the target of reactionary elements on the political Right. Of course, this narrative ignored the fact that Jack's assassin, Lee Harvey Oswald, was a committed communist, not a right-winger. But Bobby and Ted brushed aside this inconvenient truth—each for his own reason.

Bobby was tormented by guilt. He could not shake off the suspicion that his enemies in organized crime were responsible for his brother's assassination. As chief counsel to the Senate rackets committee in the 1950s and, later, as attorney general, Bobby had waged a crusade against Sam Giancana, the Chicago Mafia boss, and Jimmy Hoffa, the Mobbed-up president of the International Brotherhood of Teamsters. Bobby had expected these men to come after *him*, to retaliate against *him*—not against Jack.

After Jack's murder, Bobby carried a copy of Edith Hamilton's *The Greek Way.* In it, he had underlined a comment by the fifth-century historian Herodotus: "All arrogance will reap a harvest rich in tears. God calls men to a heavy reckoning for overweening pride." In his struggle to overcome the crushing weight of his survivor's guilt, Bobby underwent a dramatic transformation; he shed his persona as a nasty and vindictive person—Jack's "hatchet man"—and assumed the idealized persona of his dead brother.

Ted had a different perspective. To Ted's way of thinking, Jack had been martyred because of his efforts to unlatch the door of opportunity for millions of Americans. Therefore, Ted felt he had the obligation to take up his brother's unfinished work by redefining the meaning of liberalism. As Ted saw it, this new liberalism was not merely a pragmatic approach to change, like FDR's New Deal or Lyndon Johnson's Great Society. Rather, it was a moral attitude toward life, a sympathetic posture in favor of the underdog—women, blacks, the poor, and the disabled. In Ted's mind, these minorities were entitled to *preferential* treatment.

Ted's brand of liberalism, unlike JFK's, was forged in the crucible of the anti–Vietnam War movement. "Starting with anti-war feeling . . . —'make love, not war'—the young Americans picked up the anti-capitalist animus of the Marxist 1930s, and merged these emotions with either primitivism or nihilism, depending on temperaments," wrote Columbia University professor Jacques Barzun in his monumental work *From Dawn to Decadence—1500 to the Present.* "Some of the rebels formed communes in which they lived like early Christians or nineteenth-century utopian groups—brother-and-sisterhoods with property and workload in common; others hid in basements to make bombs and blow up business by way of advertising their views. . . . A . . . protest, at one of the leading universities in California, is to be remembered . . . for the slogan . . . the crowd chanted during the demonstration: *'Western Civ. has to go!'* "[14]

For Ted, as for many antiwar demonstrators, America was a sick and violent society that had to atone for the sins of genocide against Native Americans and for the oppression of women, blacks, and other minority groups. The purpose of liberal reform "was to begin to even the historical score against those who had previously tilted the game unfairly in their own favor."[15]

Ted was not alone in his belief that a bill had come due on America's guilt. In the 1960s and '70s, many people agreed with him that Americans had to pay for their complicity in the death of the young president. To a significant degree, Lyndon Johnson built the edifice of the Great Society—his ambitious and wildly expensive program aimed at eradicating poverty and racial injustice—on the foundation of the nation's collective culpability for JFK's assassination. Many worthy things were accomplished under the banner of guilt—most notably, the Civil Rights Act of 1964 outlawing racial segregation in schools, public places, and employment, and the

Voting Rights Act of 1965 eliminating discriminatory election practices against African Americans.

When, some years later, Americans finally awoke from their
Kennedy-induced reverie, they found, like Rip Van Winkle, that they
did not recognize their own country. Out of the youth rebellion, the
sexual revolution, feminism, and the other protest movements of
the 1960s, a new America had been born. In many ways, it was a better America. Certainly, it was a more fluid, open, and egalitarian
America. But it was also a coarser America, a country beset by violence, crime, and drugs and dominated by members of an antiestab-
lishment culture who adopted new ways of talking, acting, and
dressing.

"When one could go to a shop and buy . . . jeans ready-made
with spots and patches, cut short and unraveled at the edges, a new
intention was evident," wrote Jacques Barzun. "When young women
put on an old sweater, pearls, and evening pumps together, when
young men went about in suits of which the sleeves covered their
hands and the legs of the trousers were trod underfoot, they made
known a rejection of elegance, a denial of feminine allure, and a
sympathy for the 'disadvantaged.' Such clothes were not cheap;
their style was anti-property, anti-bourgeois; it implied siding with
the poor, whose clothes are hand-me-downs in bad condition. To
appear unkempt, undressed, and for perfection unwashed, is the key
signature of the whole age."[16]

The swift and ferocious cultural upheaval proved too much for
many Americans, who blamed liberals for ruining their country. The
once-solid (and conservative) South abandoned the Democrats for
the Republicans, as did millions of suburbanites who were anxious
to hold on to their comfortable, if increasingly quaint, version of the

American Dream. Ethnic blue-collar voters, until then the backbone of the Democratic Party, were repulsed by the counterculture; many in their ranks turned into the Silent Majority and voted for Richard Nixon as president—the first of several politically cautious, fiscally conservative presidents who broke with the big-government model of the liberal welfare state.

Thus, instead of advancing their cause, Ted Kennedy and the mythmakers of Camelot inadvertently encouraged the excesses of the counterculture. They were responsible for pushing liberalism to the fringe of American political life, where its influence on policy became marginal. In the forty-six years between John F. Kennedy's assassination and Barack Obama's inauguration, the Democratic Party would control the United States Senate for all but thirteen years. And yet, during most of that time, the political label "liberal" would be held in disrepute, and Ted would find himself in the ideological wilderness.

To his credit, he never gave up. He never abandoned his convictions or principles. On the contrary, he became a more effective politician. His position as odd-man-out on the floor of the Senate forced him to develop legislative skills, which, in time, enabled him to achieve incremental progress toward many of his liberal goals. Like a member of another famous political family, John Quincy Adams, who served in the House of Representatives after he was defeated for a second term in the White House, Edward Kennedy "earned the respect of his bitterest foes," and became "as great a master of parliamentary procedure as any member of Congress in history."[17]

7

ON JUNE 19, 1964—one full year after President Kennedy had sent a special message to Congress, declaring passage of the Civil Rights Act as "imperative"—the United States Senate finally took up consideration of the bill. It meant the world to Ted Kennedy, who exhorted his colleagues to pass the legislation in honor of his brother's memory. After hours of interminable wrangling over procedural details, the senators finally began voting at 7:40 P.M. As soon as the bill passed, Ted rushed from the chamber to a car that was waiting to take him to the airport. He was expected in West Springfield, Massachusetts, where the Democrats were holding their state nominating convention. Ted was running unopposed for a full Senate term, and several hundred overheated, boozed-up delegates were milling around, impatiently anticipating his imminent arrival.

But first, Ted instructed his driver to stop at Arlington National Cemetery. At the Eternal Flame in front of his brother's gravestone, he knelt on one knee, crossed himself, and took a moment to read the words of Jack's inaugural address, which were engraved in the stone. We do not know what he did next, but without straying too far from the known facts, we might reasonably assume that Ted informed his brother of the events that had just transpired in the United States Senate, the passage of the Civil Rights Act, the historic consummation of John F. Kennedy's presidency.

Not long afterward, at 8:35 P.M., a twin-engine Aero Commander 680 took off from Washington's National Airport with Senator Kennedy and three other passengers on board: Senator Birch Bayh of Indiana; Bayh's wife, Marvella; and Ted's legislative aide, Ed Moss. The pilot, Ed Zimny, warned Ted that there were thunderstorms all the way from New York City north to western Massachusetts, and that they were in for a rough flight. When the plane began to pitch and roll in the dense fog, Zimny suggested that he divert the plane to another airport.

"It was like flying through a black void," Bayh said later.[1]

But Ted was hours behind schedule and in no mood for further delays. "Damn it," he snapped at Zimny, "we're late already."[2]

In an act of bravado, Ted unfastened his seat belt and half stood, half crouched in the low-ceilinged plane. Moments later, the Aero Commander plowed into an orchard three miles from Barnes Municipal Airport, instantly killing the pilot and Ed Moss.

JEAN HEARD THE news on the 11:00 P.M. radio," said Rose Kennedy. "She crossed the street [at the Kennedy Compound in Hyannis Port] and told Bobby, who was at home in bed, and they left immediately for Ted—without disturbing their parents. So the seventh and the eighth child were a great blessing for the ninth."[3]

When Ted regained consciousness in Cooley Dickinson Hospital in Northampton, Massachusetts, Bobby was at his bedside. Looking up at his brother, Ted said, "Is it true that you are ruthless?"[4]

Three vertebrae in his lower spine were fractured, one of them almost completely crushed. Two ribs were broken. His lung was punctured. His blood pressure was almost negligible. Doctors were not at all confident that he would live through the night.

After a press conference the next day, Bobby had lunch with the columnist Jimmy Breslin. "I was just thinking back in there," he said, pointing to Ted's room. "If my mother hadn't had any more children than the first four [Joe, Rosemary, Kathleen, and Jack], she would have nothing now."[5]

Later, Bobby went for a walk with his friend Walter Sheridan, a federal investigator whom Bobby had hired in the Justice Department to help him expose Jimmy Hoffa. "We just lay down in the grass," Sheridan said, "and he said, 'Somebody up there doesn't like us.' "[6]

The following day, the paralyzed Joe Kennedy was wheeled into Ted's hospital room. His six-foot-two, two-hundred-thirty-pound son had been transferred from an orthopedic stretcher called a Stryker frame to a larger Foster frame—a pipe-and-canvas-sling contraption in which he was continually rotated, like a chicken in a rotisserie, so that the force of gravity could exert pressure on different muscles of his body without, at the same time, moving his spine. His father looked first at his son's feet, then at his face, and then at his entire body.[7]

"You should have seen [Joe's] face," said a member of the hospital staff. "His eyes were wet and pained."[8]

When the doctors recommended back surgery, Joe, who could

not articulate words, made his feelings unmistakably clear by moaning and groaning and storming at the doctors. He was too impatient to communicate by writing words on a pad.

"Dad doesn't like doctors and doesn't believe half of what they say," Ted remarked later.[9]

DESPITE HIS PARALYSIS and aphasia, Joe Kennedy wasted no time putting his formidable publicity machine to work on behalf of his injured son. As in the case of Jack's health problems, Ted's injuries were treated as an opportunity to create a positive political spin. The aim was to drape Ted in the mantle of Jack's high-minded leadership. Newspaper stories described how such eminent Harvard professors as the economist John Kenneth Galbraith and Jerome Wiesner, JFK's science adviser, came to the hospital to conduct private seminars for Ted as he slowly rotated in his Foster frame. The public was treated to a peek at Ted's highbrow reading list—a biography of Franklin Delano Roosevelt, the collected papers of the Adams family (which claimed two presidents), and Winston Churchill's multivolume history of World War II.[10] To further the resemblance between Ted and his dead brother, Ted took up one of Jack's favorite pastimes: painting landscapes. And like Jack, who had famously written *Profiles in Courage* while recuperating from back surgery, Ted was hard at work putting together a book of reminiscences, titled *The Fruitful Bough,* about his father.

"When we grew a little older," Bobby wrote in the book, "we realized that [our father] wasn't perfect, that he made mistakes, but by that time, we realized everyone did."[11]

Eleven days after his accident, while he was still recovering in Cooley Dickinson Hospital, Ted received a phone call from the man who had succeeded his brother in the White House, President Lyndon Baines Johnson.

> *LBJ:* My friend, I'm sure glad to hear your voice.
>
> *Kennedy:* . . . I wanted to call and tell you how much we appreciate it—Joan appreciates everything you've done.
>
> *LBJ:* I haven't done anything, but I'm sure ready and willing.
>
> *Kennedy:* You sent all those wonderful people up from the Army—[Deputy Secretary of Defense Cyrus] Vance did, and they made a great deal of difference and everyone's been so kind down there and they've taken great care of me. Really coming along now. Making some progress.
>
> *LBJ:* You got a bad break, but my mother used to tell me that things like that develop character and it'll make you stronger when you get older. [*chuckles*]
>
> *Kennedy:* I don't know about that. You're ready to trade a little of that. . . . That's what I keep reading in all that mail. They say you get down on that back a little while and think and do a little suffering, you'll be a better man.[12]

IN MID-DECEMBER, TED emerged from the hospital wearing a cumbersome back brace. His father's PR campaign had succeeded: many people believed that Ted's painful months in the Foster frame had turned him into a new and better man—someone who was mature beyond his thirty-two years. That, of course, remained to be seen. But one thing was certain: his near-death experience and miraculous recovery *had* turned him into a living legend.

In January 1965, when he and Bobby (who had won a Senate seat from New York) were sworn in together, the spectators in the

Visitors Gallery burst into cheers. The next day, Ted was greeted on the floor of the Senate as a conquering hero.

"The junior senator from Massachusetts will be written in history as one of the great men," said Birch Bayh, who, at the risk of his own life, had crawled back into the burning plane to pull the badly injured Ted Kennedy from the wreckage. Leverett Saltonstall, Ted's Republican colleague from Massachusetts, said, "I have admired the courage, the morale, the patience, and the frustration he has undergone in the hospital." And Daniel Inouye of Hawaii, who lost an arm in battle during World War II, rose to declare that Edward Moore Kennedy, "our beloved junior senator from Massachusetts," should have his own chapter in his brother's *Profiles in Courage*.

8

On BASTILLE DAY, July 14, 1967, Joan Kennedy gave birth to her third child. (Three years earlier, she and Ted had had a stillborn baby boy, who was buried in the Kennedy plot at Holyhood Cemetery in Brookline, Massachusetts.) The new baby, Patrick Joseph Kennedy II, was named after his great-great-grandfather, who had come to America from Ireland in 1848 and who died of consumption on November 22, 1858—105 years to the day before the assassination of John F. Kennedy.[1]

Ted and Joan's Georgetown townhouse could no longer accommodate their crowded household—three children (Kara, Teddy Jr., and Patrick) under the age of eight plus a nanny and a housekeeper. After looking at existing homes, Ted decided to build a new house on a six-acre tract of land in McLean, Virginia, near his brother Bobby's place at Hickory Hill.

For an architect, he chose John Carl Warnecke, who had designed Ted's house in Hyannis Port, Bobby's pool house at Hickory

Hill, and President Kennedy's gravesite at Arlington National Cemetery. Jack Warnecke was more than the unofficial Kennedy family architect; the tall, handsome, divorced architect and the recently widowed First Lady Jacqueline Kennedy had conducted a secret romance for quite some time, and had only broken it off the previous Christmas when Jackie started seeing Aristotle Onassis.[2]

The 12,500-square-foot house that Warnecke designed at 636 Chain Bridge Road in McLean cost more than $750,000 (nearly $5 million in today's dollars). It had a thirty-two-foot-high living room with a magnificent view of the Potomac River and the wooded banks on its other side. Approached from the outside, the gray-shingled house with peaked roofs looked like a New England country home. Inside, it was a different story. Joan worked with society decorators Keith Irvine and Thomas Fleming, who furnished the living room with an old English mantel, an antique Turkish rug, and five sofas upholstered in yellow-and-white chintz.

"The master bedroom suite is in a wing all of its own," reported Dorothy McCardle on the women's page of the Sunday *Washington Post.* "It includes a paneled den and a very masculine bathroom for Teddy, a very feminine, rose-hued bath–dressing room next door for Joan, and a huge bedroom with its own fireplace. The bedroom walls are covered with white silk moiré."[3]

By THE TIME the house was completed, it was the spring of 1968, and Ted was caught up in a fierce family debate over whether Bobby should follow the lead of Senator Eugene McCarthy, a hero of the anti–Vietnam War movement, and challenge President Lyndon Johnson for the Democratic nomination. Ted was initially opposed to the idea. And he believed that if his father were still at the top of his game, and could communicate, he would advise, "Don't do it."[4]

But once President Johnson took himself out of contention, Ted changed his mind. He tried to talk Eugene McCarthy into withdrawing from the race in favor of Bobby. And when that did not work, Ted joined his brother-in-law Steve Smith as one of Bobby's campaign managers.

From then on, Ted was absorbed by his brother's campaign. Bobby won the Indiana primary with 42 percent of the vote to 27 percent for McCarthy. The same day, Bobby beat Vice President Hubert Humphrey, 2 to 1, in the District of Columbia primary. A week later, Bobby won in Nebraska. Then it was on to Oregon, where Bobby suffered a stunning defeat at the hands of McCarthy's legions of antiwar supporters. Next up was California, a must-win state for Bobby if he was going to convince party leaders that he was a viable candidate in the fall.

Under all this pressure, Ted was drinking heavily again. Stories of his escapades with women on the campaign trail made their way back to his home at 636 Chain Bridge Road and to Joan Kennedy. It turned out that Ted's near-death experience in the plane crash and his months of painful recuperation had not, as widely advertised, turned him into a new man.

None of this came as a surprise to Joan. Two or three years before, she had read in *Women's Wear Daily* that Ted was having an affair with Amanda Burden, an ethereal blond socialite, who had recently married Carter Burden, a multimillionaire descendant of Commodore Cornelius Vanderbilt. "It was quite well known that [Ted] was having an affair with a married woman," Joan later said. "At that point, Rose Kennedy came up to me [in Palm Beach] and said, 'My dear, you can't believe any of these things you are reading. Women chase after politicians.' "[5]

But Joan found it impossible to take Rose's advice. In despair, she turned more and more to drink. She had probably inherited a genetic predisposition to alcoholism from her parents, and people began to notice that she was often unsteady on her feet. Sometimes she stumbled and fell. Her breath often smelled of alcohol. She saw a psychiatrist, who prescribed tranquilizers.[6]

"It wasn't my personality to make a lot of noise," Joan said. "Or to yell or scream or do anything. My personality was more shy and retiring. And so rather than get mad or ask questions concerning the rumors about Ted and his girlfriends, or really stand up for myself at all, it was easier for me to just go and have a few drinks and calm myself down as if I weren't hurt or angry. I didn't know how to deal with it. And unfortunately, I found out that alcohol could sedate me. So I didn't care as much. And things didn't hurt so much."[7]

9

T HAT WAS A rough affair, that rally," said David Burke, Senator Ted Kennedy's right-hand man, recalling a June 1968 campaign event in San Francisco that featured Ted as the main speaker. "There were a lot of unfamiliar faces, a lot of people who were pushing and shoving. . . . There was no sense of control. And people kept yelling and screaming things that had nothing to do with Robert Kennedy's victory [in that day's California Democratic primary], and I felt frankly uncomfortable for Edward Kennedy. I told him we ought to get out of there, and we did as soon as possible.

"We drove back to the Fairmont [Hotel]," Burke continued, "and went to our suite up there on the fourth floor, and of course the first thing we did was turn on the television set in the living room to get the latest [primary voting] results and see what was happening down there in LA. The instant the set lit up we heard someone say there's been a shooting at the rally. I assumed, and I think Edward

Kennedy assumed, that the rally they were talking about was the one we had just left. . . .

"As we were listening, we saw Steve Smith on the screen asking people, over and over, to be calm and be quiet and leave the auditorium. We knew, of course, that he hadn't been at our rally. This was Los Angeles, and there had been a shooting down there.

"And then there was the sudden, horrible dawning realization that Robert Kennedy had been shot.

"The senator didn't say anything. There was no outcry. The one reaction I remember most vividly was that there was no reaction at all.

"Ted Kennedy stood in the middle of the living room, staring at the screen. I stood beside him, unable to say anything. I heard him say, 'We have to get down there.' That was all. We just stood there, the two of us, staring at the screen, watching this thing unfold. I don't know how long we stood there; it may have been thirty seconds or it could have been three to ten minutes. We were just frozen there, because we were learning things that were more horrible all the time.

"Finally, the senator spoke. 'I want to go to Los Angeles.' "[1]

AT THE HOSPITAL of the Good Samaritan in Los Angeles, Ted was greeted by the members of his brother's inner circle—Bobby's wife, Ethel, who was two months pregnant with her eleventh child; press secretary Pierre Salinger; speechwriter Ted Sorensen; singer Andy Williams; and aide Edwin Guthman. At the end of a long hallway, Ted entered Bobby's hospital room. His brother lay on the bed, a bullet in his brain. Surgeons had tried to save him, but to no avail. A priest was called to administer the last rites, and then Bobby was gone.

After several minutes alone with his dead brother, Ted opened the door, and orderlies came in and lifted the corpse onto a stretcher and began strapping it down. As they finished their task, Ted went into the bathroom.

"Ted leaning over the washbasin, his hands clutching the sides, his head bowed," recalled one of Bobby's aides. "I never expect, for the rest of my life, to see more agony on anyone's face. There are no English words to describe it."[2]

Ted and his best friend, John Tunney, who was now a congressman from California, accompanied the gurney to an elevator for the ride down to the hospital's autopsy room. The elevator stopped at a lower floor, and Allard Lowenstein, a liberal activist who had initially backed Eugene McCarthy against Robert Kennedy in the primaries, got on.

"I felt I shouldn't be there," recalled Lowenstein, who had stuck with Eugene McCarthy even though his sympathies were with Bobby. "But there was no way I could get off, nothing I could do." As the elevator reached the basement and Bobby's body was wheeled off, Lowenstein turned to Ted Kennedy and said, "Now that Bobby's gone, you're all we've got. . . . Take the leadership."[3]

SEVERAL DAYS LATER, Ted found himself standing in front of an overflow crowd in New York City's St. Patrick's Cathedral, delivering his brother's eulogy: "My brother need not be idealized, nor enlarged beyond what he was in life. He should be remembered simply as a good and decent man, who saw wrong and tried to heal it, saw war and tried to stop it. Those of us who loved him and who take him to his rest today pray that what he was to us, and what he wished for others, will someday come to pass for all the world."[4]

Ted was inconsolable. Now he was truly alone, the last surviving son of his father's dynastic schemes, the last surviving father of his brothers' children, the last surviving hope of many who were knocking insistently on the door of Opportunity—the blacks, the poor, the women, and the young.

WHEN HE BURIED his brother under a Japanese magnolia tree in Lot 45-A, Section 30 of Arlington Cemetery, not far from the grave of President Kennedy, Ted Kennedy was thirty-six years old, just one year over the constitutionally imposed age for the presidency. The White House had been his father's dream and his brothers' dream, but it had never been *his* dream.

"Never, never did Teddy want the job [of president], no matter what he said publicly," insisted his friend Senator George Smathers of Florida. "Some politicians need recognition, some thrive on being in a more important position. It's food for them. Ted Kennedy grew up with power all around him. . . . He didn't need more power. He didn't need to be a bigger shot than what he already was."[5]

Nonetheless, his father had once told him, "If there is a piece of cake on the plate, take it! Eat it." And so, despite all his reservations, Ted began his long, uncertain, conflicted journey in pursuit of the presidency—a pursuit that would last for the next twenty years.

A draft-Ted movement began immediately. Chicago's Mayor Richard Daley, who controlled the powerful Illinois delegation, and who intended to play the role of kingmaker at the Democratic National Convention that summer in the Windy City, launched a campaign to draft Ted for the number-two spot on Hubert Humphrey's presidential ticket. Ted told Mayor Daley that he had no interest in the vice presidency. Next, Larry O'Brien—Jack's old campaign manager, who was now working for Humphrey—called Ted. "Are you available to run with Hubert?" he asked. "No" came the answer from Ted, who said he was busy sailing.

But then Ted said something that threw the Democratic Party into a state of confusion. In his first public appearance since Bobby's assassination, he gave a speech at Holy Cross College in Worcester, Massachusetts, that was covered by all the major television networks. "There is no safety in hiding," he declared. "Not for me; not for any of us here today; and not for our children, who will inherit the world we make for them. . . . Like my brothers before me, I pick up the fallen standard. . . ."[6]

The speech was a bombshell. "Lyndon Johnson heard it, and decided Ted was planning a coup [at the convention]," wrote the *Times*' Adam Clymer. "Daley heard it, and called to raise the idea of Ted running for President, not Vice President as he had urged before."[7]

In late August, Steve Smith—the tough-minded Kennedy brother-in-law who ran the family's finances and its political campaigns—told R. W. "Johnny" Apple of the *New York Times*, "No one is going to find a shred of evidence that the senator is working for the nomination." At the same time, however, Smith confided to friends that Ted did not have to work for the nomination; it was his for the asking. And Smith was not alone in that view. The California delegation was ready to bolt for Ted. Senator Russell Long had lined up the Louisiana delegation behind Ted. And William vanden Heuvel, who had been Bobby's assistant at the Justice Department, was so sure that Ted could win the nomination that he phoned him in Hyannis Port and urged him to declare his availability.

"You know," vanden Heuvel said, "this is a long hill, the presidency. It's a hard hill to climb, and all I'm saying to you, and I'm not trying to persuade you, is that the nomination in my judgment is yours, if you're willing to be available to it. And I'm not pressuring you in any way, but it will probably be a long time before we're ever this far up the hill again."[8]

But again, the answer from Ted was the same firm "No." His friends and political associates were confused. Ted was not talking like a Kennedy. Had he forgotten Joe Kennedy's First Commandment: "If there's a piece of cake on the table, take it!"?

Ted had his reasons for not wanting to run. Chief among them, he said, was that "this was Bobby's year."[9] "The remark," wrote the *New York Times*' William Honan, "alludes to an interesting fact about the relationships in the Kennedy family; namely, that although his brothers were competitive with each other, they also accepted their places in a rigid hierarchy. The elder's 'rightful' place always was on top. This meant Ted could compete against Bobby vigorously, but he could not triumph over his older brother without feeling guilt for having upset the hierarchy, and when this situation arose Ted would immediately set about to restore Bobby's position of supremacy by making disparaging jokes about himself or otherwise permitting Bobby to get on top again.

"When Bobby was killed," Honan continued, "Ted felt not just grief, but guilt—guilt for having triumphed over (by surviving) his older brother, a guilt that could not be assuaged by putting Bobby back up where he had been. The fact that Ted was then offered the prize his brother was seeking, and been cheated of by an assassin, only compounded his guilt feelings."[10]

After the Democratic Convention nominated the ticket of Hubert Humphrey for president and Edmund Muskie for vice president, Ted felt he owed it to the party to assist in the presidential campaign. "Accordingly, he wanted to send two emissaries to the candidates," said Lester Hyman, a trusted Kennedy operative from

Massachusetts. "He had chosen Kenny O'Donnell [President Kennedy's chief of staff] and me for the assignments. He gave me a choice between Humphrey and Muskie. Knowing how notorious Hubert was for talking and talking and talking, with total disregard for schedules, often late into the night, I decided that it would be less frustrating for me to go with Muskie, although I never had met the man. I almost immediately packed my bags and set off on a new adventure as the Kennedy representative to the Muskie campaign."[11]

In the meantime, Ted sat down for a wide-ranging interview with Warren Rogers of *Look* magazine and expanded on his reasons for resisting a draft: "How could I conscientiously combat allegations by Nixon—and we had to anticipate he would make them—that I was too young, that I had no record in public life strong enough to recommend me for the high office of President, and that perhaps I was trying to trade on my brother's name."[12]

Implied but not stated: Ted Kennedy planned to use the next four years to create a record in the United States Senate that would make him eligible for the office of president.

PART TWO

"Something Terrible Is Going to Happen"

10

————

T ED WAS NOT the only one looking ahead to 1972. The voice of the Establishment, the *New York Times*, was running stories that cast Ted Kennedy as Richard Nixon's all-but-inevitable opponent the next time around.[1] In fact, the editors of the *Times* were so certain that Ted would challenge Nixon in 1972—and become a prime target for assassination—that they updated his obituary and set it in galley proofs.

Ted professed not to care; he was not afraid to die. "If someone's going to blow my head off," he said, "[I want] just one swing at him."[2] But that was his bravado talking. He lived with the fear that he would be the next Kennedy brother to go.

The weight of responsibility was more than Ted could bear. It paralyzed him. A month after Bobby's assassination, he got into his car in McLean, Virginia, and drove to the Capitol with the intention of returning to his desk on the floor of the Senate. But he could not get out of the car, and he drove home. He spent time at his house on

Squaw Island with Joan and their three children, Kara, Teddy Jr., and Patrick. But their father hardly said a word to them; he walked right past them as though they didn't exist. He sought solace in the sea, sailing a rented yawl all the way up to Maine. He did not bathe; he did not shave; he hardly ate. When he came back to Hyannis Port, he looked in on his parents.

"Dad rose up in his chair, his eyes wide, pointing a finger at me. . . ." Ted said. "I didn't know what was wrong—the old sweater I was wearing, or something. I went over to kiss him, and he held up his hand and put it on my chin. It wasn't much of a beard, a couple of weeks or so. But I hadn't had a haircut the whole time. My mother threatened to shave off the beard herself right there, but I did it. We all had a good laugh afterward, and, seeing my father laugh like that at last, my mother said, 'I wish we could do this every day.' "[3]

Ted thought about quitting politics. Asked by Joe Mohbat of the Associated Press whether he could stand up to party demands that he run against Richard Nixon in 1972, Ted replied: "Damn right I could, in an instant. I honestly don't feel any obligations to pick this one up. . . . [Campaign events] pretty much turn me off now. When I first came into this in 1962, it was really good, easy. But the kicks aren't. . . . I mean, meeting Molly Somebody and hearing about her being Miss Something. . . . What's it all for? I used to love it. But the fun began to go out of it after 1963, and then, after the thing with Bobby, well. . . ."[4]

TED'S COMPULSIVE WOMANIZING and drinking were subjects of persistent gossip on Capitol Hill. Many of his colleagues expressed concern that Ted was headed for a crack-up. But back then, reporters did not write about such intimate personal matters; they believed public figures should be judged solely on the substance of their performance, not on the morality or immorality of their personal lives.

A particularly revealing—and unreported—incident occurred during a trip that Ted took in April 1969 with a group of fellow senators to Alaska. The purpose of the trip was to gather facts about the conditions of impoverished Indians, Eskimos, and Aleuts. On the way home, Ted began drinking from Bobby's silver hip flask. "First time I've used it," he told writer Brock Brower. He soon became wildly drunk and started running up and down the aisles of the plane, shouting "Es-ki-mo Power!" Aides tried to quiet him down, but he would not listen. "They're going to shoot my ass off the way they shot Bobby," he said. "They're going to shoot my ass off the way they shot Bobby. . . ."[5]

At Dulles Airport, a large crowd had gathered to welcome the senatorial delegation home. Joan was there with all three of her children.

"We started to get ourselves together," recalled one of the journalists. "I looked out and everybody was there all right, the TV cameras, the whole world. I left behind Kennedy and he did look awful, his eyes were like oysters on the half shell. Joan saw him and her jaw dropped four feet. I remember thinking, *That's all for you, buddy*. Then little Patrick rushed over to him, and Kennedy picked the little boy up and kissed him, and Patrick's head blocked off the cameras, and Kennedy was home free. The kid stole the show."

"John Lindsay at *Newsweek* . . . called me up after that trip," recalled Lester Hyman, a Kennedy family friend. "And he said, 'I got to tell you something. Your friend Ted Kennedy is in a lot of trouble psychologically.' And he told me about the drunken incident.

And [Lindsay] said [Ted] was just totally out of control, and he said . . . 'I really believe . . . he just can't handle things right now.' And he added, 'There's something wrong, and if [Ted] doesn't do something about it, I believe something terrible is going to happen to him.' "[6]

11

——

THAT SUMMER, JOHN Lindsay's prediction came true. On July 20, 1969, the major television networks interrupted their live coverage of astronaut Neil Armstrong's scheduled Moonwalk to deliver a news bulletin. The day before, Edward Kennedy had been involved in an automobile accident on a remote island off the coast of Martha's Vineyard. The senator had survived when his car plunged off a bridge into the water below, but a young woman riding in his car had died.

The young woman's name was Mary Jo Kopechne. She was one of the so-called Boiler Room girls who had worked as an aide to Senator Robert Kennedy in his presidential campaign. Despite their affectionate if somewhat condescending nickname, the Boiler Room girls were women of considerable substance who had demonstrated an interest in politics. Chosen for their brains and tough-mindedness, they acted as the campaign's eyes and ears, compiling intelligence reports, keeping track of primary delegates in key states, and negotiating deals on behalf of the candidate.

Of all the Boiler Room girls, Mary Jo Kopechne was the one who least resembled the picture of a brash political operative. A pretty ash blonde with a slight build (she weighed a hundred and ten pounds), she had the prim manner of a devout Catholic schoolgirl. For a time, she had considered becoming a nun. She enrolled in Caldwell College for women, a school run by the friars, nuns, and sisters of the Dominican Order. After she graduated with a degree in business administration, she moved to Montgomery, Alabama, to teach impoverished black children at the Montgomery Catholic High School. But eventually, her dedication to social and political activism led her to Washington, D.C., where she ended up working for Robert Kennedy.

"Mary Jo Kopechne was among the most highly regarded [of Bobby Kennedy's aides]," wrote Burton Hersh, a writer who was closer to the Kennedys than most journalists. "She herself worked exhaustively with Bob's staff, spent one whole night typing his decisive breakaway Vietnam speech at Hickory Hill, traveled on his behalf— they knew each other well enough to share Kennedy-style 'in' jokes, banked, like so many Kennedy jokes, off such drolleries as those of a prominent Louisiana politico whose silk suits and shirts and alligator shoes left both of them giggling."[1]

Though all of the Boiler Room girls were deeply committed to Bobby's presidential crusade, none showed greater passion than Mary Jo. While the other women occasionally took time off to be with their boyfriends, Mary Jo, who was approaching her twenty-ninth birthday, appeared to live a celibate life. After her death, her parents would claim that Mary Jo had been planning to marry a member of the Foreign Service. But that statement came as news to her friends. As far as they could tell, Mary Jo had never had a serious relationship. If she was ever in love with a man, it was Bobby Kennedy—but only in a platonic way.

"After Bob died, there was a great deal of sadness cleaning out his headquarters," said Joey Gargan, a cousin and boyhood chum of Ted Kennedy's who had worked on Bobby's campaign. "The girls who worked so hard were devastated, like all of us were. [Mary Jo] was very hurt by Bobby's assassination, deeply wounded."[2]

That first summer after Bobby's assassination, Joey Gargan invited Mary Jo and eleven other Boiler Room girls to Hyannis Port to give them a "break in this sad ordeal." For three days, they swam and sailed and reminisced about Bobby. Ted Kennedy was too distraught to attend, though Joan Kennedy put in an appearance. The women had such a good time that, a year later, Joey asked Ted if they could repeat the Boiler Room girls' reunion during the 1969 Edgartown Regatta.

"Gee," Ted said, according to Joey Gargan, "that would be lots of fun. Let's do it."

THE WEEKEND OF Chappaquiddick, [Ted] and I flew up to Boston, and then down to the Cape together," said Thomas "Tip" O'Neill, who had replaced John F. Kennedy in the House of Representatives when Kennedy moved over to the Senate. Years later, O'Neill recalled that on the shuttle to Boston, Ted had talked about personal matters, including the Edgartown Regatta, in which he planned to race his brother Jack's boat, the *Victura*. He mentioned to Tip that Joey Gargan was urging him to go to a party for the Boiler Room girls, and that he, Ted, did not want to go, but felt obliged to show the flag. And then, seemingly out of nowhere, Ted turned to Tip and said: "Jeez, I've never been so tired in my life."[3]

At one o'clock in the afternoon on Friday, July 18, 1969, Ted arrived on Martha's Vineyard, exhausted and strung out. He was met by his driver, Jack Crimmins, a foulmouthed grouch, who took Ted to Chappaquiddick Island, a short ferry ride across from Edgartown. There, in a modest two-bedroom cottage that had been rented by Joey Gargan for the reunion party later that night, Ted changed into a bathing suit. Then he and Crimmins drove down a narrow paved road onto the rough gravel of Dike Road and over a narrow, ramshackle seventy-five-foot-long hump-backed bridge and out to East Beach, where Mary Jo and the other Boiler Room girls were frolicking in the water.

The Edgartown Regatta began at three o'clock, and the Boiler Room girls—Mary Jo, Esther Newberg, Susan Tannenbaum, Rosemary "Cricket" Keough, and the sisters Nance and Maryellen Lyons—watched the race from a boat that had been rented for the occasion by Paul Markham, a former U.S. attorney for Massachusetts and, like Joey Gargan, a Kennedy acolyte. Ted Kennedy's boat came in ninth in a field of thirty-one.

By nine o'clock that night, everyone was at the rented cottage on Chappaquiddick Island. Altogether, there were twelve partygoers—six Boiler Room girls and six men, including Ted Kennedy, Jack Crimmins, Joey Gargan, Paul Markham, and two Kennedy advance men, Charles Tretter and Raymond La Rosa. The fact that all the women were young and single and most of the men were married and without their wives would later raise a number of eyebrows.

"The mood was kind of mixed," recalled Charles Tretter. "I remember listening to the girls, the long string of reminiscences I myself wasn't really privy to, anecdotes, stories that came out of the Bobby campaign. What I'm getting at is, I worked for [Ted Kennedy] for a long time, and I think I know him pretty well, well enough to realize that he was—he was not exuberant. He was not having a helluva good time."

Tretter continued: "There was getting to be long lapses in the evening, people were standing up and Kennedy was working hard at being a good host. If there was a girl not saying much he would try and draw her out. It was just that the conversation, what was said— *Bobby*. He was a presence."[4]

Afterward, there were contradictory accounts of the amount of alcohol consumed at the party. "It was a steak cookout, not a Roman orgy," insisted Esther Newberg. "No one was drinking heavily." But Joey Gargan painted a different picture. He said that Paul Markham was drinking heavily, as was Ted Kennedy's chauffeur, Jack Crimmins.

"Jack had become his usual arrogant self, as only he can get after five or six Scotches," said Gargan.[5]

The curmudgeonly Crimmins was eager that everyone leave the cottage. "Get all these douche bags out of here," he said. "I want to get some sleep. The last ferry leaves at twelve o'clock. I want everybody out."

"Jesus, Jack," Ted Kennedy said, "you're stiff! How am I going to get home?"

"Take a fucking cab!" Crimmins replied.

"They talked that way to each other all the time," Gargan said. "It sounded hostile, but it really wasn't. And here you have another party, and Ted is kidding Crimmins again, because Jack's had quite a few. And Jack is saying, 'Get these broads out of here. I want to go to sleep. I don't give a shit how you get home, Kennedy. I'm not driving you.' And the senator's saying, 'Okay, Jack. That's what we're doing. We're going. We're leaving right now.' "[6]

Ted Kennedy asked Crimmins for the keys to his car. He was going to drive himself back to Edgartown, and he was taking Mary Jo with him.

. . .

. . .

It was now nearing midnight, and Ted had been drinking steadily for nearly eight hours, since the conclusion of the regatta. He later claimed he had had only five rum-and-Cokes, or about ten ounces of alcohol. But people familiar with his binge drinking doubted those figures. If Ted had been behaving true to form, he would have consumed at least ten to fifteen drinks in that amount of time. It was well known among his friends that Ted became tipsy after only two drinks, so he was almost certainly drunk when he left the party with Mary Jo. However, that fact was never officially established, because the police did not test his blood-alcohol level after the fatal accident. Even if they had, it wouldn't have done them much good, since Ted delayed his appearance at the police station long enough for his body to have metabolized most of the alcohol.

When Mary Jo left the party with the senator, she was wearing a white long-sleeved blouse, dark slacks, sandals, two bracelets, and a ring. However, she didn't have her pocketbook with her—a curious omission for a woman as fastidious as Mary Jo. Nor did she ask Esther Newberg, her roommate for the weekend, for the key to their room at the Katama Shores Motor Inn in Edgartown. In short, Mary Jo behaved as though she planned to return to the party after a brief midnight rendezvous with Ted Kennedy.

At the time, no one paid much attention to her departure. But later, her friends expressed astonishment that a devout Catholic like Mary Jo, whose morals had never been questioned, had disappeared into the night in the company of a married man with the lecherous reputation of Ted Kennedy. It wasn't like Mary Jo to go "for a roll in the hay," as one writer put it. But Dr. John J. McHugh, the Massachusetts State Police chemist, provided a possible explanation for Mary Jo's behavior. He tested the alcohol content of Mary Jo's blood after her death. It measured .09 percent, which Dr. McHugh said "would be consistent with about 3.75 to 5 ounces of 80- to 90-proof liquor within one hour of death." That meant Mary Jo, who had little experience with alcohol, had at least two or more drinks during the last hour of the party.

"At that rate," wrote Robert Sherrill in his exhaustive 1974 investigation of Chappaquiddick for the *New York Times Magazine,* "Ms. Kopechne would appear to be perhaps the heaviest drinker at the party—assuming that the others were telling the truth about their own alcohol consumption."[7]

As TED AND Mary Jo pulled away from the cottage, he was behind the wheel of his four-door Oldsmobile Delmont 88. Under the best of circumstances, when he was stone-cold sober, Ted was a terrible driver. He paid no attention to posted speed limits, and he often forgot to look out the windshield while he was talking to the person in the passenger seat. Apparently, his driving skills were no better that night, for instead of turning left on Chappaquiddick Road and heading toward the Edgartown ferry slip, he made a sharp right turn onto the gravel of Dike Road—the very same road that his driver Jack Crimmins had taken earlier in the day when he drove the senator to the swimming beach. Just before the hump of the rickety Dike Bridge, Ted's Oldsmobile crashed through the shallow railing and plunged into Poucha Pond.

The Olds flipped over onto its roof and sank under six to seven feet of water. According to Ted's later testimony, he somehow managed to wriggle out of a car window and claw his way to the surface for air. Then, he claimed, he made seven or eight attempts to dive down and rescue Mary Jo. Only after his efforts proved futile did he leave the scene and stagger the mile and a quarter to the rented cottage. On his way, he passed a summerhouse. Some of the lights were on inside the house, where there was a telephone that Ted could have used to call the police.

"There's been a terrible accident," Ted told Joey Gargan and Paul Markham when he got back to the cottage. "The car's gone off the bridge down by the beach, and Mary Jo is in it."[8]

Instead of immediately notifying the police, Gargan and Markham acted on an impulse to protect Ted Kennedy. The three men got into a white Plymouth Valiant and raced to the scene of the accident. On the way, Ted was sobbing, "This couldn't have happened. This couldn't have happened. What am I going to do? What can I do?"[9]

Arriving at the bridge, Gargan and Markham saw the upside-down Oldsmobile submerged in the water.

"As soon as I saw that, I got sort of butterflies in my stomach," Gargan said. "I realized if Mary Jo was in that car, there was no hope. I said to myself, 'Oh, shit, this is over! This is done. She's gone.' "

Nonetheless, Gargan and Markham stripped off their clothes and dove into the cold water. The strong current flowing through the channel nearly swept them away.

"All I was interested in was saving the girl; I wasn't thinking about anything else," Gargan said. "I felt there was only one thing to do, and that was get into that car as quickly as possible. Because if we didn't, there was just no chance in the world of saving Mary Jo."[10]

From the shore, Ted Kennedy called out several times: "Can you see her? Is she there?"[11]

Gargan looked across the dark surface of the water. Framed in the headlights of the Plymouth Valiant, he could see the senator, lying on his back. He was rocking back and forth and moaning: "Oh, my God. What am I going to do?"

When it became apparent that rescue was impossible, Gargan

and Markham helped Ted Kennedy into the Valiant, and they headed for the Edgartown ferry slip.

"There was a discussion—'What do we do now?'—that was done in a sort of half-trance, like sleepwalking," Gargan said. "We were all stunned; we were all horrified. We were discussing the situation, trying to decide what to do, trying to get the story together prior to reporting the accident. The accident is over. We're reporting the situation now. How that was to be done."

Leo Damore, whose 1988 book *Senatorial Privilege: The Chappaquiddick Cover-Up* is still considered the definitive account of the accident and its aftermath, interviewed scores of people associated with the tragedy. Among them was Joey Gargan, who broke the Kennedy code of *omertà* to give Damore his version of events.

"The senator was silent about his intentions, but it appeared he did not want to report the accident at this time," Damore wrote on the basis of his interviews with Gargan. "Kennedy was having alternative ideas about the situation: Why couldn't Mary Jo have been driving the car? Why couldn't she have let him off, and driven to the ferry herself and made a wrong turn?

"Kennedy asked to be brought back to the cottage to establish the story," Damore continued. "After a while he could leave. Kennedy suggested that when he was back at the Shiretown Inn [where he was staying in Edgartown], Gargan could 'discover' the accident and report to police that Mary Jo had been alone in the car. How this was going to be worked out insofar as 'details' were concerned, the senator didn't say."[12]

Gargan had never before refused to do his cousin Ted's bidding. Orphaned in childhood, he had been raised by his aunt, Rose Kennedy, who taught him that his chief role in life was to take care of Ted, regardless of the price to be paid or the effort needed. But this time, Gargan flatly refused to assume responsibility for Ted's screwup. He would not make a false report to the police and risk losing his license to practice law. As the three men pulled up to the ferry landing, Gargan suggested that they go together to the Edgartown police station and report what had happened.

"As we drove down that road," Ted later recalled, "I was almost looking out the front window and windows trying to see her walking down that road. I related this to Gargan and Markham, and they said they understood this feeling, but it was necessary to report it. . . .

"All right, all right, Joey!" Ted yelled at Joey Gargan. "I'm tired of listening to you. I'll take charge of it. You go back. Don't upset the girls. Don't get them involved."

And with that, Ted leaped from the car, took a few steps, and dove off the pier into the narrow channel of water that separated Edgartown from Chappaquiddick Island. Fully clothed, he began swimming across the inlet to the far shore, where the ferry landing looked deserted. Gargan jumped out and watched him go.

"I hope he drowns, the son of a bitch!" Gargan mumbled under his breath.[13]

Later, Ted recalled his nocturnal swim: "I started to swim out into that tide and [I] . . . felt an extraordinary shove . . . almost pulling me down again, the water pulling me down and suddenly I realized . . . that I was in a weakened condition, although as I had looked over that distance between the ferry slip and the other side, it seemed to me an inconsequential swim; but the water got colder, the tide began to draw me out, and for the second time that evening, I knew I was going to drown. . . . And after some time, I think it was the middle of the channel, a little further than that, the tide was much calmer, gentler, and I began to . . . make some progress, and finally was able to reach the other shore. . . ."[14]

. . .

. . .

Back at the Shiretown Inn, Ted Kennedy exchanged his wet clothes for dry ones and lay down on the bed to collect his thoughts. He had made it back safely, without the ferry operator or any of the motel employees seeing him. That was good, because it would allow him to claim that he was in Edgartown when the accident occurred on Chappaquiddick.

In an apparent effort to nail down his alibi, he went to the lobby and found Russell Peachy, the innkeeper. He told Peachy that a noisy party had awakened him from sleep. Then he made a point of asking Peachy for the time. It was 2:55 A.M., Peachy replied. With that time firmly established in Peachy's memory for use in any future police investigation, Ted returned to his room. He slept for a few hours, then showered, shaved, and dressed in fresh yachting clothes.

At some point that morning, he began placing a rapid-fire se-ries of phone calls—seventeen in all, many of them charged to his credit card. Perhaps the most important was to attorney Burke Mar-shall, one of Bobby's assistants at the Justice Department and a man known to the Kennedy family as a "defuser of blockbusters." It was Marshall who had represented the Kennedy family in its successful effort to bowdlerize William Manchester's book *The Death of a President.*

At eight o'clock in the morning, Gargan and Markham showed up at the Shiretown Inn. They were eager to hear directly from Ted what he had told the police. Instead, they found him on the porch, casually chatting with a group of friends as though nothing was wrong.

"What happened?" Gargan asked when they were behind the closed door of Ted's room and safely out of earshot of the others.

"I didn't report it," Ted admitted.

"What the fuck is going on?" Gargan screamed. "You were supposed to report the fucking accident."

It soon dawned on Gargan that, despite his strenuous objections the night before, Ted had expected him to take care of things. That was what Joey was supposed to do—regardless of the price to be paid. As far as Ted was concerned, Joey should have told the police that Mary Jo, not Ted Kennedy, had been driving the fatal car.

"This thing is worse now than it was before," Gargan said. "We've got to do something. We're reporting the accident right now."

"I'm going to say that Mary Jo was driving," Ted insisted.

"There's no way you can say that!" Gargan said. "You can be placed at the scene."[15]

Even then, however, Gargan and Markham did not take Ted Kennedy to the police station to report the accident. Instead, the three men returned to Chappaquiddick Island to make some phone calls and decide on their next step.* There, they ran into some of the Boiler Room girls—Esther Newberg and the Lyons sisters— walking toward the ferry landing. Gargan assembled everyone back at the cottage and told them that Ted had been in an automobile accident and that Mary Jo was "missing."

"Can't you do something?" Nance Lyons asked. "Isn't there some way we can have somebody else as driver of the car?"

"That would be impossible," Gargan said.

"I don't know why *you* couldn't be driving the car," Nance

---

*More than ten years later, on March 12, 1980, the *New York Times* ran a front-page article headlined GAPS FOUND IN CHAPPAQUIDDICK PHONE DATA. The *Times* reported: "Records of Senator Edward M. Kennedy's telephone calls in the hours after the accident at Chappaquiddick were withheld by the telephone company from an inquest into the death of Mary Jo Kopechne without the knowledge of the Assistant District Attorney who asked for them."

Lyons said, looking at Joey Gargan. "Can't somebody else take the blame?"

"We can't, that's all!" Gargan fired back. "The senator was driving."[16]

BY THEN, TWO amateur fishermen had notified Edgartown police chief Dominick J. "Jim" Arena that they had spotted the wrecked car in Poucha Pond. Chief Arena summoned John Farrar, an expert scuba diver on the Edgartown Search and Rescue Squad. On one of his first dives, Farrar located Mary Jo's body in the well of the backseat of the Oldsmobile. The body was stiff with rigor mortis. Her hands clasped the backseat. Her face was turned upward.

"It looked as if she were holding herself up to get a last breath of air," Farrar said. "It was a consciously assumed position."[17]

Farrar tied a rope around Mary Jo's neck, so that her body would not be swept away by the tide as he pulled it to shore.

"She didn't drown," Farrar said later. "She died of suffocation in her own air void. It took her at least three or four hours to die. I could have had her out of that car twenty-five minutes after I got the call. But he [Ted Kennedy] didn't call."[18]

Dr. Donald R. Mills, the on-duty medical examiner, and Eugene Frieh, a local undertaker, examined Mary Jo's corpse. At the funeral home, Frieh removed Mary Jo's clothes—the white long-sleeved blouse, the dark slacks, the sandals, the two bracelets, and the ring.

By now, Chief Arena had traced the license plate on the wrecked car to its owner—Edward M. Kennedy. When he called the police station to order the officer on duty to find the senator, he was informed that Ted was already there.

"I am sorry," Chief Arena told Ted when the senator came to

the phone. "I have some bad news. Your car was in an accident and the young lady is dead."

"I know," Kennedy replied.

IN HIS STATEMENT to the police—which Ted dictated and Paul Markham wrote out in block letters—the senator declared: "When I fully realized what had happened this morning, I immediately contacted the police."

That, of course, was not true. More than nine hours had transpired between the time of the accident and the time Ted showed up at the Edgartown police station. And although Ted admitted he had driven the car in which Mary Jo lost her life, he admitted little else. He did not, for instance, mention the fact that he and Mary Jo had attended a party, along with five other women and five other men, at which alcoholic beverages had been served. He did not mention that the party guests were still on Chappaquiddick Island, and could be interviewed as witnesses by the police. He did not mention that Joey Gargan and Paul Markham had tried to rescue Mary Jo instead of summoning the police for help. He did not mention that, after Gargan and Markham failed to bring up her body, they still did not call the police.

About three o'clock that afternoon, Ted Kennedy, Joey Gargan, and Paul Markham were driven in police cruisers to the Martha's Vineyard airport, where they boarded a chartered plane and flew to Hyannis Port. The Boiler Room girls were hustled off the island without being interviewed by the police. Mary Jo's body was embalmed and prepared for shipment to her parents' home in Pennsylvania. No autopsy was ever performed.

The news of Mary Jo's death was being carried by the wire services by the time Ted arrived in Hyannis Port. He went to see his paralyzed father to tell him what had happened.

"I was in an accident, Dad, and a girl [died]," he said. "That's all there was to it, but you're going to be hearing a lot about it on TV." Then, covering his face with his hand, he sobbed, "I don't know, Dad. I don't know. . . ."

Over the next several days, family consigliere Steve Smith, freshly back from a vacation in Majorca, assembled a group of Kennedy loyalists at Ted's home on Squaw Island—speechwriters Theodore Sorensen, Milton Gwirtzman, and Richard Goodwin; Kennedy son-in-law Sargent Shriver; Ted's political guru David Burke; two of Ted's closest friends, Senators John Culver and John Tunney; former defense secretary Robert McNamara; and former assistant attorney general Burke Marshall. In addition, Steve Smith hired no fewer than nine attorneys, including Edward Hanify, who had powerful political connections in Massachusetts.

However, it was the presence of the legal heavy-hitter Burke Marshall that alerted the media to the fact that the Kennedys were treating a motor-vehicle case like a major political crisis. Over the next several days, scores of reporters descended on the Kennedy Compound, demanding that Ted hold a press conference and explain himself. Burke Marshall nixed the idea.

"The reason I thought he should not make a statement to the press," said Marshall, "was that I did not know enough about his legal situation. A lawyer's instinct with his friends and clients is to shut up. Politically, it was a bad thing, I suppose. . . ."

"Our prime concern," Steve Smith explained, "was whether the guy [Ted] survived the thing. Whether he rode out the still-possible charge of manslaughter."

Dick Goodwin, who was the savviest member of the group

when it came to handling the press, did not agree with the gag rule imposed by Marshall and Smith. Goodwin was in favor of getting the full story out as quickly as possible. But, said Goodwin, Ted was "obviously panicky still. Obviously really shaken up, and yet nobody else was really willing to make the kind of serious decisions a situation of this sort required. We had there a great, headless, talented monster. Nobody could decide what to do. So, finally, by the middle of the week they transformed it into a political problem, which they could deal with. . . . [T]hey were trying to say something and still avoid the connotation of immorality—the old Irish Catholic fear of ever suggesting that you were screwing anybody outside of marriage. Drink and sex acquired a disproportionate size."

SEVERAL OF TED Kennedy's oldest friends and associates were excluded from the Squaw Island crisis team, a slight they naturally resented. When they got wind of the confab, they tried to reach Ted to offer their advice.

"I called out there," said family friend Larry Newman, "and got Joan. I said, 'Joan, will you get a message to Teddy?' She said, 'Larry, how can I get a message to him when they won't let me talk to him?' "

"No one told me anything," Joan said later. "Probably because I was pregnant, I was told to stay upstairs in my bedroom. Downstairs, the house was full of people, aides, friends, lawyers. And when I picked up the extension phone I could hear Ted talking to Helga [Wagner, a former German airline stewardess with whom Ted was having an affair]. Ted called his girlfriend Helga before he or anyone told me what was going on. It was the worst experience of my life. I couldn't talk to anyone about it. . . . Nothing ever seemed the same after that."[19]

Lester Hyman, the Democratic operative with close ties to the

Kennedys, was at his home in the Berkshires when he heard the news about Chappaquiddick.

"I called down to Hyannis Port to see how [Ted] was getting on," Hyman recalled, "and I got Dick Goodwin. He was the first person I talked to, and he sort of brushed it off. Then I talked to another one. . . . And I'll never forget it so long as I live. I said, 'Look, obviously from what you are all telling me, Ted is in shock. That's what it sounds like to me. And if I were you, I would immediately have him go to the hospital so he can have time to recover from this shock, and then discuss things, instead of you all being down there. . . .' And the answer to me was, 'Oh, don't worry. It's a one-day story.' "[20]

But Chappaquiddick was a story with legs. *Newsweek* ran a cover story, based in large part on a memo that its Washington correspondent, John Lindsay, had written after Ted's drunken Alaskan trip the previous April. The story said that the senator's "closest associates" had been "powerfully concerned over his indulgent drinking habits, his daredevil driving, and his ever-ready eye for a pretty face." This broke new ground; no one had ever written anything as personal as that about a Kennedy before.

At the time of Chappaquiddick, Jack Kennedy had been dead for nearly six years, but his closest political associates still dreamed of a Kennedy Restoration. Until now, they had looked upon Ted Kennedy as the vehicle that would carry them back to power. But now Ted had dashed their hopes, and one of Jack's closest friends and advisers, Ted Sorensen, found it hard to forgive him.

Sorensen's ambivalent feelings for Ted were on full display in a speech he crafted for the senator. For the first time, words seemed to fail Sorensen. In one draft, he had Ted Kennedy declare: "I will never follow the path of my brothers, I will never seek the presidency." But the Kennedy sisters objected, and the phrase was excised. The final

Sorensen text was full of holes and contradictions and evasions and unnecessary admissions and bloated rhetoric. It created far more problems than it solved.

"There is no truth, no truth whatsoever, to the widely circulated suspicions of immoral conduct that have been leveled at my behavior and [Mary Jo's] regarding that evening," Ted said in his fifteen-minute televised speech that was carried live by all three television networks on July 25, 1969. "There has never been a private relationship between us of any kind. . . . Nor was I driving under the influence of liquor. . . .

"All kinds of scrambled thoughts . . . went through my mind," he continued, "whether the girl might still be alive somewhere out of that immediate area, whether some awful curse did actually hang over all the Kennedys, whether there was some justifiable reason for me to doubt what had happened and to delay my report, whether somehow the awful weight of this incredible incident might in some way pass from my shoulders. I was overcome . . . by a jumble of emotions—grief, fear, doubt, exhaustion, panic, confusion, and shock."

Then, Ted made an urgent plea to "the people of Massachusetts." Looking directly into the camera, he asked his constituents to send him their "advice and opinion" on whether he should stay in public life or resign his seat in the Senate. The appeal was an echo of Richard Nixon's demagogic 1952 Checkers speech, in which Nixon took his case directly to the American people via television in order to remain the running mate of presidential candidate Dwight Eisenhower. Ted's aides later referred to this part of his speech as "send in your box tops."

"Almost anything he could have said would have been better than what did happen," said Dick Goodwin. "He did the worst thing he could have, he Nixonized the situation."

Nonetheless, Ted's appeal was successful. As he and Ted Sorensen had hoped, thousands of phone calls, telegrams, and letters poured into Ted's office, urging him to remain in the Senate.

In NOVEMBER 1969—four months after Chappaquiddick—Joe Kennedy began refusing nourishment, and the Kennedy family gathered in Hyannis Port for the deathwatch. Jackie, now married to Aristotle Onassis, flew in from Greece to be near Joe during his final hours. There, in Joe's room, she found Ted in a sleeping bag on the floor.

"If God does not take him straight to heaven, I will be really mad at God," Jackie said after Joe died on November 18. "Look how valiant and loving he [was] in all this sickness."

"Joe Kennedy put the first Catholic in the White House," said family friend Eddie Dowling. "In my book, this would make him the greatest man of accomplishment in all history. . . . Here is a man who didn't understand failure. It doesn't make any difference what it is. If it's a train you've gotta catch, catch it. . . . If you're sent out to get a loaf of bread, come back with a loaf of bread. . . . If he said to you, '. . . at one o'clock tomorrow, Wednesday, the thirteenth of November, I'm going to be at the South Pole,' he'd be there, at the South Pole. . . . he'd find a way to get there. This is the kind of training [his] boys have had."

JOSEPH KENNEDY'S DEATH spared him the pain of the official inquest into the death of Mary Jo Kopechne. The inquest was held in January 1970 in Edgartown, the Dukes County seat. Ted Kennedy and twenty-six other witnesses were called to testify at the closed inquest. Among them was Deputy Sheriff Christopher "Huck" Look, who testified that he had seen Ted and Mary Jo in Kennedy's car at the intersection of Dike Road and Main Street more than an hour *after* Ted claimed he had left the party. Deputy Look's testimony cast serious doubt on the timeline of Ted's story.

Deputy Look testified that between 12:30 and 12:45 on the morning of the accident, he had seen the headlights of a car coming toward him near the curve at the intersection of Dike Road.

"Knowing the road, I slowed down because there's a sharp corner that people will cut too close," Look said. "I wanted to make sure I didn't get sideswiped."

Deputy Look was "positive there was a man driving, and a woman next to him. . . . I observed in my rearview mirror that the car was parked, and it looked like they were going to back up. I thought they wanted information, that they were lost or something. . . ."[21]

Look pulled over and got out of his car and walked toward the other car. When he was twenty-five to thirty feet away, the car took off down Dike Road in a cloud of gravel and dust. The driver of the car appeared to be in a "confused state," Look said. The deputy sheriff made a mental note of the license plate: it began with an "L" and contained the number "7"—both details that were found on the license plate of Ted's 1967 Oldsmobile Delmont 88.

The judge presiding over the inquest, Massachusetts district judge James A. Boyle, concluded that Ted had lied about where he was taking Mary Jo when they left the party. "I infer," wrote Judge Boyle, ". . . that Kennedy and Kopechne did not intend to return to Edgartown at that time." In addition, Judge Boyle found "probable cause to believe that Edward M. Kennedy operated his motor vehicle negligently . . . and that such operation appears to have contributed to the death of Mary Jo Kopechne."

Nonetheless, Dukes County district attorney Edmund S. Dinis chose not to seek an indictment for involuntary manslaughter. Instead, Ted got off with a two months' suspended sentence and the temporary loss of his driver's license.

. . .

Two months after the inquest, in March 1970, Leslie Leland, the Dukes County grand jury foreman, requested that the jury be convened to investigate the death of Mary Jo Kopechne.

"We weren't out to get Kennedy," Leland said. "We just wanted to get to the truth."

However, District Attorney Edmund Dinis blocked Leland's efforts to subpoena key witnesses, including Ted Kennedy, Joey Gargan, Paul Markham, and the five surviving Boiler Room girls. Leland then asked to see the transcript of the inquest. But that request was denied him as well.

"I was dejected," Leland said. "We had tried to do our job, to get at the truth, but we couldn't."

"There was definitely a cover-up," said another grand juror, Lloyd Mayhew. "We were all madder than hell that we couldn't subpoena anyone we wanted. Our hands were tied."

Although Ted managed to escape Chappaquiddick with the lightest possible legal slap on the wrist, the Kennedys blamed Joey Gargan even for that. He had failed in his role as Ted's Protector. No one was angrier with Joey than Rose Kennedy. After Chappaquiddick, Rose ordered her attorney to cut Joey out of her will—the severest form of punishment she could think of. Rose later relented and wrote Joey back into her will, but Ted banned Joey from all further involvement in his political and personal life.

"As long as my mother's alive, you can come over to see her," Ted told Joey. "But you have to ask first. If I'm here, you can't come over. And after she dies, you can never come again."[22]

However, as time passed, Ted softened and let bygones be

bygones. He invited Joey and his family to the Kennedy Compound, where the two men embraced each other again like brothers.

"Ted has helped Joey," said a close friend of the family. "One of Joey's children had serious medical problems, which Ted has very generously taken care of. He also arranged for Joey to move to a bigger house in Hyannis and to keep the bungalow in Hyannis Port for his kids when they are in town."[23]

BOBBY'S WIDOW, ETHEL, had been given the sensitive task of calling Mary Jo's parents, Gwen and Joseph Kopechne, who lived in Pennsylvania, and telling them that their daughter was dead.

"I'll never forget her words," Gwen Kopechne recalled many years later in the last interview that she and her husband would ever give.* "Ethel said, 'God has a plan for us all, and Mary Jo is in her rightful place in heaven.'

"At the funeral," Gwen Kopechne continued, "Ethel took my arm, and I held on to it so hard I'm sure it was black and blue. But Ethel and Rose seemed to understand our pain. Rose kept in touch with us for over a year. At one point, she invited us to New York, to her apartment, saying she was going to have us for dinner."

For a moment, Gwen fell silent, and Joseph Kopechne took up the story.

"Much of the time we were there in New York, Rose was cleaning her windows with Windex and a cloth," he said. "She apologized, but said she was so upset that the windows were dirty, she couldn't leave them that way. We were pretty amazed to see her

---

*Joe Kopechne died in 2003 at the age of ninety. Gwen died four years later at age eighty-four in the Valley Nursing Home in Plains Township, Pennsylvania. They were buried next to Mary Jo in St. Vincent's Cemetery in Larksville, Pennsylvania.

scrubbing away. You felt like you should pitch in, but we just sat there, not quite knowing what to do. Then, after she ordered some sandwiches, she came out wearing a new dress. She was sort of modeling the dress, and she wanted to know how she looked."

Gwen said, "Young Teddy Jr. wrote us several letters over the years. He was just a little boy at the time, but they were very heartfelt and honest. Of course our hearts went out to him for losing his leg, and to his parents as well. The letters really sounded as though he had written them on his own. He wrote that he had met Mary Jo, and had liked her very much. He said she had always paid attention to him, even though he was a little boy surrounded by busy adults, who usually ignored him. There was a lot of sensitivity and emotion in those letters.

"Twice after Mary Jo's death, Ted had us come to his house in McLean, saying he wanted to talk to us," Gwen went on. "But unlike the visit to Rose, which was strange but warm, it was uncomfortable—for all of us. Ted led us to believe he was going to explain what really happened. But when the time came, after plenty of small talk, he said he just couldn't talk about it. It was very puzzling. Twice we drove all the way down there, and twice he couldn't talk about how our daughter died."

The burden of guilt sat on Ted's chest like an anvil. He desperately wanted to relieve himself of the guilt, but in the end, he couldn't find the words to express his feelings. And, in fact, he would never find expiation for his guilt.

For years to come, Chappaquiddick would be the inextinguishable underground fire of American politics. Every time Ted Kennedy thought the blaze had been stamped out—and that he was free at last to run for president—it would flare up again, smoldering and belching its noxious fumes as intensely as ever. Eventually, the fire burned itself out, and the memory of Chappaquiddick began to disappear into the mists of history. By the time Ted Kennedy was diagnosed with brain cancer in 2008—nearly forty years after Chappaquiddick—the median age in America was 35.3 years, and most people no longer immediately associated the name Ted Kennedy with Chappaquiddick.

Still, Chappaquiddick had a lasting impact. At the time of Chappaquiddick, Ted was probably the only figure in the Democratic Party who could have healed the rift between the Old Left (with its focus on the Cold War, union activism, and other economic issues) and the insurgent New Left (with its focus on the anti-Vietnam War movement and the values of the counterculture).

"A great historic opportunity to pull the Democratic Party together was lost," observed political analyst William Schneider. That lost opportunity had profound consequences. With the Democratic Party torn by ideological fratricide, the stage was set for the long conservative ascendancy in American politics.

Moreover, Chappaquiddick ensured the reelection of President Richard Nixon, and the continuation of the unpopular Vietnam War, along with the war's casualties—both physical on the battlefield and psychological back home. Chappaquiddick gave Nixon the excuse he had long been looking for to spy on his political enemies. As will be explained later in this book, he hired private detectives to gather damaging information on Ted Kennedy—the first in a series of illegal acts by Nixon that ultimately led to Watergate and Nixon's resignation from the presidency.

The blow from Chappaquiddick shattered the gentlemen's agreement that had existed between reporters and politicians and had restrained journalists from covering the private lives of public figures. Chappaquiddick opened the way for a new, more cynical school of journalism, one that took particular delight in exposing the feet of clay of well-known people. After Chappaquiddick, nothing in American life was sacrosanct, not even the glittering legend of Camelot, and Camelot's last living legatee, Edward Kennedy.

PART THREE

"A Second Chappaquiddick"

12

___

ON TED KENNEDY'S first DAY back in the United States Senate following Chappaquiddick, Majority Leader Mike Mansfield made a public display of greeting him warmly and escorting him to his desk. But Mansfield's gesture did little to sweeten the reception Ted received from his colleagues.

Among the one hundred senators in the 91st Congress, fifty-seven were Democrats and forty-three were Republicans. There was only one woman, Margaret Chase Smith of Maine, and one African American, Edward Brooke of Massachusetts. Many senators, both Democrats and Republicans, had once flocked to Ted Kennedy's committee hearings and press conferences to bask in his celebrity and get their faces on TV. Now, after Chappaquiddick, a number of them went out of their way to avoid being seen in his presence.

Few senators were in a position to cast the first stone, and in time, a number of them would achieve their own public infamy. Herman Talmadge of Georgia would be "denounced" by the Senate for his unethical conduct; John Tower of Texas would fail to be confirmed as secretary of defense because of his extramarital affairs and heavy drinking. Harrison A. Williams of New Jersey would be convicted of taking bribes in the Abscam sting operation. And Ted Stevens of Alaska would be convicted of seven felony counts for failing to report illegal gifts (though the decision would eventually be reversed following revelations that the prosecution had withheld evidence).

It was an open secret that many senators sexually harassed their female staffers, that others tried to seduce young female interns, and that still others sold their votes in return for campaign donations. The most powerful senator in the 91st Congress—Richard Brevard Russell Jr. of Georgia—was a white supremacist and unapologetic segregationist, which didn't stop his colleagues from naming a Senate office building after him.

Without doubt, many senators derived pleasure in flaunting their righteous indignation over Ted Kennedy's behavior on Chappaquiddick Island. But there was also a tinge of envy in their sanctimony. *It's about time,* these senators seemed to be saying, *that the Kennedys got their comeuppance.*

WITH HIS COLLEAGUES' disrespect came diminished influence. Many bills that Ted Kennedy supported—on health care, tax reform, gun control, and a lowered voting age—went down to defeat. His vulnerability invited petty personal attacks by his political opponents. They held hearings to consider a bill that would have changed the name Cape Kennedy back to Cape Canaveral. The proposal did not pass, but the fact that such an affront to the assassinated president could even come up for consideration in the United States Senate indicated just how far Ted's star had fallen. Dejected, depressed, and stressed out, Ted fell ill with pneumonia.

Much of Ted's power had derived from his position as heir presumptive to the presidency. But now, even his political allies questioned his right to succeed his brother Jack. Ted Sorensen said that Senator Kennedy "recognizes that his prospects were damaged [by Chappaquiddick] if not destroyed." And Arthur Schlesinger Jr. added: "I think that with Chappaquiddick the iron went out of Edward Kennedy's soul."

There was talk that Ted would resign from the Senate. And in his darkest hours, he mulled over that possibility with family and friends. But as long as he remained a senator, he was determined not to hang his head in shame. In his role as the Senate majority whip, he ranked second only to Majority Leader Mansfield, and it was his duty to appear on the Senate floor and round up the necessary votes.

"Teddy wanted to be seen," said Wayne Owens, an aide on his whip staff. "In two weeks, he had turned a little bit from the ultimate celebrity to the ultimate curiosity. So, process-wise, at twenty to twelve, I would come to the Senate office and brief him on what was happening that day . . . because we had a press conference . . . every day with Mike Mansfield. And Teddy was at those press conferences. . . .

"And then we would just kind of hang around, slipping off into the cloakroom or into the lobby or something. . . ." Owens continued. "But he made the decision to get right back on the bucking horse, right back out in public. He was never any shrinking violet. And those times were really tough because one of my tasks frankly was watching the wire stories to see whether [Dukes County district attorney] Edmund Dinis . . . had indicted him or something, had figured out a way to get the grand jury to indict him.

"And then since his [driver's] license had been suspended, I would drive him home at night. I mean these were really tough, mean times for him. And yet, his old Irish dark sense of humor was wonderful, and he loved stories on Chappaquiddick. You know, if I would hear a good Chappaquiddick joke, he would always want to hear it. He would say, 'What, get any new jokes or any new lines?' "[1]

I RARELY TAKE the Capitol subway—only when it's raining terrifically hard," Ted Kennedy said several months after Chappaquiddick. "I like to walk whenever I can and go by both where Jack's office was and where Bobby's office was. I can remember different things Bobby said as I pass by the places where we stood and talked. When I go by the north entrance hall, I think of President Kennedy delivering his inaugural address there and I remember that was where the country honored him in the end."[2]

The *New York Times* reporter who recorded Ted's words was sufficiently moved to reflect upon their meaning. "What was evident from such talk," the reporter wrote, "was that beaten and humiliated as Kennedy then was, forced as he was to contemplate the possibility of dropping out of public life altogether, he still loved the Senate—loved it as a young priest loves his church."[3]

The decision whether to remain in the Senate was not his alone to make; he had to consider its impact on his family. Since Chappaquiddick, there had been a noticeable increase in threats against his life and the lives of his wife and children. Police cruisers were now stationed twenty-four hours a day outside his home on Chain Bridge Road on the Virginia side of the Potomac. The Secret Service escorted his children to school and brought them home at the end of the day. The pressure on Joan proved to be too much; she suffered a miscarriage—the second in their ten-year marriage.

"What if I didn't run again?" Ted asked Fred Dutton, a Democratic strategist. "What if I retire?"

"Well, do you have anything in mind?" Dutton asked.

"Maybe return to law practice in Boston," Ted said. "Maybe see if I can buy the *Boston Herald*. Maybe sit in the south of France."

But in the end, Ted couldn't bear to lose his identity. *He was a man of the Senate.* And so, as the election season of 1970 approached, he dusted himself off and announced that he was indeed running for reelection. He was determined to run as hard as or harder than he had the first time around.

"The voters need reassurance," he told R. W. Apple of the *New York Times*. "They need to see me, to be convinced that I'm reliable and mature. You can't counter the Chappaquiddick thing directly. The answer has to be implicit in what you are, what you stand for, and how they see you."

The voters also needed to see Joan Kennedy campaigning by his side. It would be a signal that his wife had forgiven him for Chappaquiddick, and that it was all right for the voters to forgive him, too. Joan agreed to campaign, but her heart wasn't in it. Ted didn't really need *her;* he needed a *symbol.*

"I felt used rather than needed," Joan told one interviewer. And to another, she admitted: "That's when I truly became an alcoholic."[4]

Ted raised $1.2 million—a considerable sum for a senatorial race in those days. A good deal of that money was spent on registering young voters. The effort paid off in the fall, when he won the election to a third term with a comfortable 62 percent of the vote.

He had weathered the Chappaquiddick storm in his home state. But on January 21, 1971, he was handed a humiliating defeat in the Senate. Several Democratic senators who had privately promised to vote for him in his reelection bid as majority whip failed to make good on their pledges. He lost the secret ballot to Robert Byrd of West Virginia, a former ranking member of the Ku Klux Klan.

It was, said historian James MacGregor Burns, "a second Chappaquiddick."[5]

. . .

FRIENDS WORRIED THAT Ted's defeat as Senate whip, coming as it did so soon after Chappaquiddick, would be the final crushing blow. But that was not how Ted saw it.

"There's something about me I had hoped you would understand," he told a journalist. "I can't be bruised. I can't be hurt anymore. After what's happened to me, things like that just don't touch me, they don't get to me."[6]

In fact, losing the post as Senate whip turned out to be a blessing in disguise. It freed him from the tedious business of having to round up votes and allowed him to concentrate on the real work of the Senate, which was conducted in committees. It also allowed him to travel. He gathered his wife and three staff assistants and made a five-state swing around the country. He gave anti–Vietnam War speeches that attracted large and enthusiastic crowds. Reporters noted that he wore a pair of cuff links engraved with the initials "JFK." He was acting like a presidential candidate. Newspapers began to ask: Was Ted Kennedy preparing to run for the White House in 1972?

Rose Kennedy had something to say about that. "He promised me . . . he promised me faithfully that he would not run," she said. "I told him I did not want to see him die too, that I could not stand another tragedy like the deaths of his brothers John and Bobby."

That was Rose's official position, and she stuck to it in public. But in private, Rose told Ted, "There never has been a mother of two presidents. . . . So get busy!"

13

—

F OR AS LONG as anyone in Washington could remember, Richard Nixon had been obsessed with the Kennedys. First, there was Jack, who "stole" the White House from Nixon in 1960. Then came Bobby, who might have defeated Nixon in 1968 if it hadn't been for an assassin's bullet. Now there was Ted Kennedy. There was talk that Ted was all washed up because of Chappaquiddick, but Nixon didn't buy that line. Nixon felt certain that Ted was going to run against him. The Kennedys were like vampires: Nixon would never be rid of them until he drove a stake through Ted's heart in the 1972 presidential election.

Nothing that Ted Kennedy did or said escaped Nixon's attention. The president had followed Chappaquiddick from day one. Along with millions of other television viewers, he'd been watching Neil Armstrong's *Apollo 11* spacecraft circle the Moon on July 20, 1969, when the broadcast was interrupted with the news of Ted Kennedy's accident on Chappaquiddick.

Presidential speechwriter William Safire, who'd once worked as a publicist and was sometimes called to the Oval Office for his public-relations advice, offered the opinion that the Chappaquiddick incident would be forgotten in the excitement of Neil Armstrong's Moonwalk.

"No," said Nixon, disagreeing with Safire. "It'll be hard to hush this one up; too many reporters want to win a Pulitzer Prize. . . . He [Ted Kennedy] was obviously drunk and let her drown. He ran. There's a fatal flaw in his character."

Later that same day, in a meeting with Nixon, his chief of staff, H. R. "Bob" Haldeman, scribbled notes on a legal pad as the president spoke about his nemesis, Ted Kennedy. Haldeman's notes caught the flavor of Nixon's morbid obsession:

> obviously was drunk—escaped—let her drown
>> said nothing till police got to him
>
> can't have dived & been in shock
>> ran out & slept it off—then reported
>
> really get dope on that girl [Mary Jo Kopechne] parents
>> etc.
>>> what they [Ted Kennedy and Mary Jo] doing
>>>> together etc.
>
> flaw in character
>> cheated at school
>> ran from accident—girl drowned.
>
> chance for a press guy to get a prize
> check out police chief—Mafia
>> get full check.[1]

With the president's consent, John Erlichman, assistant to the president for domestic affairs, called in Jack Caulfield, a former New York City detective who was on the White House payroll. He ordered Caulfield to send a private eye by the name of Tony Ulasewicz, one of Caulfield's former police colleagues, to Martha's Vineyard to see what he could dig up on Kennedy. (For his dirty work, Ulasewicz was secretly put on the payroll of the Committee to Reelect the President [CREEP]; he received $22,000 a year plus $1,000 a month in expenses.)

"We want to be sure Kennedy doesn't get away with this," Erlichman instructed Caulfield.

The very next day, July 21, 1969, Caulfield sent a confidential memo to Erlichman:

> The best thinking now as to the reason for the lapse in time
> between the incident and the [police] report is that Kennedy
> was very drunk and his friends were making attempts to
> sober him up prior to making the official report.[2]

That same day, Chief of Staff Bob Haldeman took notes on his ever-present legal pad during another White House discussion about Chappaquiddick:

> man up there [Martha's Vineyard]—tips
>   Sen[ator] has been playing w/ this gal couple of yrs.
> The road was no mistake
> It has been used reg. by this guy for
>   assignation purposes
> earlier in eve neighbors had complained
> ordered man & girl in car out of the area
> pressure is on up there very heavy
> but some[thing] is bound to break in spite of this[3]

Over the following days, Jack Caulfield sent regular reports to the White House:

It seems to me a thrust from here should center about an exposure of the party details, for example: The names of those attending? How many were married men? Why was the cottage cleaned bare? Where were all of the people attending the party during the early morning hours?[4]

On July 26, 1969, the day after Ted Kennedy delivered his television address on Chappaquiddick, Haldeman noted the following conversation with Republican Senate Minority Leader Everett Dirksen:

> Dirksen agree[s] [Kennedy's] influence badly impaired
> D. says now on whenever anyone sees him [Kennedy]
> there will be constant conscious[ness] of girl drowning. . . .
> K misfortune takes off some pressure
>   in Sen[ate]—no one on either side believes him
> when put to test—failed to stand up like
>   a man & no one will ever forget it[5]

Even while Nixon & Co. were plotting Ted Kennedy's political destruction, the president was feigning friendship with Ted. On August 4, 1969, after a breakfast briefing of the legislative leaders of both parties, Nixon invited Ted into his office for a private chat. Bob Haldeman was present to take notes of the conversation.

> [The president] told [Kennedy] he understood how rough it was, etc. Said he was surprised to see how hard the press had been on him, especially because they like him, but you have to realize they are your enemy at heart, even if they do like you, because their prime motivation is the story.[6]

. . .

IN THE SPRING of 1970, shortly after publication of the official inquest into the death of Mary Jo Kopechne, detective Jack Caulfield composed a memo suggesting a plan of action to undermine Ted Kennedy if he chose to run against Nixon in 1972.

On April 30, 1970, Caulfield wrote:

> [Murray] Chotiner [a political dirty trickster who had been involved in all of Richard Nixon's campaigns] and I have discussed this matter and we both agree that the media will do an initial effective exposure of the distortions. For the long haul, either this November or [the presidential election year of] '72, we can program, if need be, a very damaging document for public consumption. . . . When and if it becomes necessary, we can take the step recommended above. In the meantime, I will keep the document in my possession. It is ready for your perusal any time.[7]

Former detective Tony Ulasewicz explained the mysterious reference to a "document" in his 1990 memoir, *The President's Private Eye*. "Staff members of the Republican National Committee were kept busy clipping and pasting together every newspaper article and editorial [about Chappaquiddick] that broke into print," Ulasewicz wrote. "The White House wanted a record of the attack on Kennedy's credibility to use if Kennedy ever sought the Presidency. A scrapbook of the articles and editorials was put together and given the title 'At an Appropriate Time.' "[8]

Nixon probably never saw the scrapbook. But he liked Caulfield's idea, and during a presidential flight to Rome in September

1970, he ordered Haldeman to create a "campaign attack group." The president wanted the members of this group—Murray Chotiner, speechwriter Pat Buchanan, and political operative Lyn Nofziger, among others—to obtain the income tax returns of Nixon's potential Democratic opponents in 1972, including Ted Kennedy's.

The illegal White House campaign against Ted didn't stop there.

In December 1970, clandestine photos, taken in Paris and showing Ted carrying on with an "Italian princess," were sent by the White House to Edmund Muskie to be used against Ted in the 1972 Democratic primary.

In June 1971, according to Haldeman's notes, Secretary of State Henry Kissinger reported to Nixon that

> Teddy Kennedy is now in the position of practically being a total animal. At the opening of the Kennedy Center, he went to work on Christina Ford, whom he had also propositioned at the Carlyle. . . . He walked up to her door, said he wanted to screw her, and she said that they couldn't because of the press, and he said the press will never touch me. He pulled the same thing on Edgar Bergen's daughter [Candice]. . . . So we need to take advantage of this opportunity and get him in a compromising situation if we can.[9]

ON MAY 15, 1972, while campaigning in Laurel, Maryland, for the Democratic presidential nomination, George Wallace, the governor of Alabama, was shot by a would-be assassin. The near-fatal attack convinced many people that all presidential contenders—even those who had not yet won their party's nomination—should be given Secret Service protection, and Nixon immediately seized on this idea as a way to plant spies on Ted Kennedy.

"Is there anyone [in the Secret Service] we can rely upon?" Nixon asked Erlichman at a meeting in the Oval Office.

"Yeah, yeah," Erlichman replied. "We got several."

"Plant one, plant two guys on [Kennedy]," Nixon said. "This would be very useful."

Later, Nixon added: "We just might get lucky and catch this son of a bitch. Ruin him. . . . It's going to be fun."

And so, Nixon assigned a Secret Service detail to Ted Kennedy, even though Ted hadn't declared his candidacy for the nomination and hadn't asked for protection. Perhaps smelling a rat, Ted called off the protection after a few weeks.

IN THE END, Ted Kennedy decided not to run in 1972, and Nixon scored a landslide victory over his ineffectual Democratic opponent, George McGovern. Several months after the election, James McCord, one of the burglars convicted of breaking into the Democratic National Committee's headquarters at the Watergate office building in Washington, D.C., wrote a letter to U.S. District Court Judge John J. Sirica. In his letter, McCord charged the Nixon administration with covering up the Watergate conspiracy. His letter helped set off the Watergate investigation that consumed the country for the next two years.

On March 13, 1973, Nixon met in his office with John Dean, the White House counsel. During their long, rambling conversation, which was secretly tape-recorded by the president, Dean and Nixon discussed a strategy to counter the Watergate investigation being conducted by his Democratic adversaries in Congress.

Dean informed the president that William Sullivan, the former head of the FBI's domestic intelligence operations who had been fired for insubordination by FBI director J. Edgar Hoover, had come forward with an offer of help. Sullivan was prepared to blow the whistle on Nixon's Democratic predecessors—Presidents Kennedy and Johnson—for using illegal means to spy on American citizens. For instance, Sullivan could testify that he had personally mailed tapes in 1964 to Coretta Scott King containing secret recordings of her husband, Martin Luther King Jr., with other women.

Nixon was curious to know what Sullivan wanted as a quid pro quo for his cooperation.

"He wants back in the Bureau very badly," Dean said.

"That's easy," Nixon replied.

However, for reasons that have never been explained, Nixon did not give Dean permission to unleash William Sullivan against Nixon's enemies. Instead, Dean and Nixon got sidetracked on a different subject—the illegal $100,000 slush fund from CREEP that had been used to pay for the dirty-tricks campaign against Ted Kennedy.

> *Dean:* There is a certain domino situation here. If some things start going, a lot of other things are going to start going, and there are going to be a lot of problems if everything starts falling. So there are dangers, Mr. President. I'd be less than candid if I didn't tell you the—there are . . .
>
> *President:* I see . . .
>
> *Dean:* [Y]ou'll recall that sometime . . . right after Chappaquiddick, somebody was put up there [on Martha's Vineyard] to start observing. Within six hours.
>
> *President:* Did we?
>
> *Dean:* That's right.
>
> *President:* I didn't know that.
>
> *Dean:* That man watched that—he was there for every second

of Chappaquiddick, uh, for a year, and almost two years he worked for, uh, he worked for Jack Caulfield . . .

President: Oh, I heard of Caulfield, yeah.

Dean: . . . when I came over here [to the White House], I inherited Caulfield . . .

President: Yeah.

Dean: Well, if they get to those bank records . . . and they say, "What are these about? Who is this fellow . . . that you paid?" There comes Chappaquiddick with a vengeance. This guy is a, is a twenty-year detective on the, uh, New York City Police Department.

President: In other words, we— . . . [*unintelligible*] consider that wrong, do we?

Dean: Well . . . it's going to come out and the whole thing is going to turn around on that one. I mean, if Kennedy knew the bear trap he was walking into. . . . [The detective] talked to everybody in [Edgartown]. He's the one who caused a lot of embarrassment for Kennedy already. . . . He went up there as a newspaperman. "Why aren't you checking into this? Why aren't you looking there?"—bringing the press's attention to things. The guy did a masterful job.

President: . . . why didn't we get it [the damaging information on Ted Kennedy] out anyway?

Dean: Well, we sort of saved it. [*laughs*][10]

BUT IT WAS no laughing matter. For by now, Ted Kennedy had become aware of Nixon's machinations. To save his foundering presidency, Nixon was prepared to resort to what some were calling a "doomsday scenario." He threatened to disclose the most damaging secrets of the Kennedy administration—namely, that President John Kennedy had secretly plotted to assassinate foreign leaders and had illegally wiretapped the telephone conversations of American citizens.

Nixon had two goals in mind. First, he wanted to show that *his* abuses of power, which were known collectively as "Watergate," were no worse than those that had been committed by John Kennedy. And second, by discrediting the record of the Kennedy administration, Nixon hoped to eliminate the Kennedy mystique and undermine Ted's claim to the Democratic presidential nomination in 1976.

This time, Nixon had it right: Ted had his sights set on 1976. And Ted was under no illusions; he understood that Nixon would stop at nothing to discredit him. That left Ted with little choice: if he wanted to keep his 1976 hopes alive, he had to take on Richard Nixon.

Ted had an unusually able man to assist him in the largely sub-rosa campaign that he waged against Richard Nixon. The man's name was Jim Flug, and he was the chief counsel on Ted's Administrative Practices and Procedures Subcommittee of the Judiciary Committee. Working closely with Ted Kennedy, Jim Flug gathered a mountain of incriminating information against the Nixon administration, which was used later in the Watergate investigation.

Senate Majority Leader Mike Mansfield went along with the Kennedy-Flug probe, but Mansfield ruled that, when the time came, no Democrats with presidential ambitions could sit on the committee investigating the Nixon administration. Mansfield wanted to avoid the appearance of a partisan witch hunt. And that automatically eliminated Ted Kennedy from the public fray.

Nonetheless, Ted managed to play a vitally important, if unheralded, role in the Watergate proceedings. He made sure that Sam Ervin's Senate Select Committee to Investigate Campaign Practices, which investigated Watergate, was invested with the necessary power to do its job. He brought in his old friend Burke Marshall to monitor the House of Representatives' impeachment inquiry. Marshall in turn recommended his protégé, John Doar, to become the special counsel of the impeachment inquiry. Ted and Jim Flug rewrote key sections of the charter under which Harvard professor Archibald Cox would function as the independent Watergate special prosecutor. Cox was a fierce Kennedy partisan who had served as solicitor general in John Kennedy's administration.

And so, by 1973, the impeachment juggernaut was in the hands of many people loyal to Ted Kennedy. When President Nixon subsequently ordered Cox to be fired, Ted Kennedy called the firing "a reckless act of desperation by a president who is afraid of the Supreme Court, who has no respect for law and no regard for men of conscience." The next day, Ted put his staff to work researching the historical precedents for a Senate impeachment trial of Richard Milhous Nixon.

The embattled president never resorted to the "doomsday scenario."

14

———

IN NOVEMBER 1973, as the tenth anniversary of President Kennedy's assassination approached, tragedy struck the Kennedy family yet again. It began when Ted Kennedy's middle child, Teddy Jr., who had just turned twelve, complained of a pain in his right leg that wouldn't go away.

The boy didn't take his complaint to his father, who was absorbed by the Watergate investigation. He didn't tell his mother, either, because Joan was thousands of miles away in Europe, where, according to *Washington Post* gossip columnist Maxine Cheshire, she was "leading a life of her own." Instead, Teddy Jr. went to Theresa Fitzpatrick, his governess, who passed on the boy's concerns to Ted.

"Say what you will about Ted being self-absorbed, he was a devoted father," remarked a longtime family friend and political supporter who spoke on the condition of anonymity. "Ted told me later that he felt a chill when the governess told him that Teddy had a pain that wouldn't go away. It wasn't like Teddy to complain. Ted looked at his son's leg as he lay stretched out on his bed, and discovered a rather large, hard lump on the underside near his knee. It was unlike anything he had seen, and it set off alarms."[1]

Ted took his son to Georgetown University Hospital for X-rays. They showed that the boy had a tumor in the bone of his right leg. A biopsy was performed, and, according to one of the doctors, it revealed that the tumor was a chondrosarcoma, a cancer of the ligament, which was less deadly than an osteosarcoma, or primary bone cancer. Nonetheless, Teddy's doctors were concerned that the cancer might have spread, and they recommended that his leg be immediately amputated above the knee joint.

Ted called Joan, who flew back from Switzerland. Husband and wife were together when they broke the news to young Teddy that his right leg would have to come off. In tears, Teddy wanted to know whether he was going to die. No, no, his father assured him. With an artificial leg, Teddy would be as good as ever. He'd be able to sail and ski.

"Ted was shattered," said a friend. "Teddy Junior was actually comforting his father. The day after the surgery I came by Georgetown Hospital and gave Teddy an astronomy game from FAO Schwarz. It was about ten o'clock in the morning when Ted and Joan arrived. She had a scarf over her head but looked disheveled, which I at first thought part of her grief. But when I greeted them it was obvious she was very drunk. Her words were slurred and she couldn't walk straight without Ted's assistance. [Joan may have been on tranquilizers, which would have also explained her slurred speech and unsteady gait.]

"Obviously it added to Ted's concern. But mostly I felt the boy would feel very bad seeing his mother in that condition. Nevertheless she went in and visited him. Rose was pacing back and forth outside his room, praying out loud, and fortunately didn't appear to notice Joan's condition."

F ACED WITH THE responsibility of caring for a desperately sick son, and consoling two other children, Joan tried to pull herself together and stop drinking. She was only partly successful.

"I would get [to the hospital] at nine in the morning," she said. "Ted would come later. Little Teddy had to prepare for big Ted, to be on stage. He had to be strong for his father. He had to be a man for his father. He had to be a Kennedy. The whole Kennedy philosophy is not to dwell on your pain, and for God's sake don't be introspective, don't feel sorry for yourself. Ted would bring in the whole front line of the Washington Redskins and they would slap little Teddy on the shoulders and say, 'Tough guy, you're going to be fine.' And in the afternoon big Ted would parade all these dignitaries and nurses and this stream of people through the room to meet little Teddy. Ted really believed that we [couldn't] let the kid have one moment to himself to rest. He should be kept entertained. And this went on until finally about five or six days later little Ted said, 'I'm so tired but I can't tell Dad.' And so I had to do it.

"My whole marriage I was put in the position of being the spoilsport, but I did it for my children," Joan continued. "I promised [Teddy] I wouldn't tell Ted that his son was tired, that he just wanted to watch TV. Ted got mad at me and said I was no fun, that I didn't want my son to have a good time. I had to take it. I guarded the door and I was the traffic cop."

Though Teddy's operation was declared a success, further pathological studies revealed that the original diagnosis of ligament cancer had been misleading. In fact, Teddy Jr.'s cancer was far more serious than that. He did have osteosarcoma, primary bone cancer.

Over the winter of 1973–74, Senator Kennedy visited several cancer research centers and spoke to experts from all over the world. In March, he convened a brainstorming session of experts at his home in McLean, Virginia.

"After the four-hour meeting," recalled Richard Burke, the senator's assistant, "the consensus was that Teddy should participate in a new, still-experimental course of chemotherapy to attack any remnants of the malignancy. Every third Friday, I drove the senator to National Airport, where [he met] Teddy. No matter what the senator's mood, he was always upbeat in Teddy's presence, for he knew that the boy would already be dreading the ordeal. Father and son flew to Boston to spend the weekend at Children's Hospital Medical Center, where Teddy endured injections of methotrexate—a drug so toxic that additional shots of antidote were needed. The senator slept on a chair in Teddy's hospital room and did all he could to help. . . . The side effects of chemotherapy were severe, including nausea and hair loss. The senator made occasional remarks to me about how strong Teddy's spirit was, but I knew that the boy wavered between periods of optimism and gloom."

Watching his son suffer was more than Ted Kennedy could bear. "Sometimes I hear him crying," Ted said in April 1974. "We try to make out as though we have not noticed his sadness, but it tears the heart out of me. Now [that] the days are getting longer, he often sits at the window watching the children outside, and he cannot play with them because he is too exhausted."

TEDDY JR.'S ILLNESS put an enormous strain on a family that was already rent by deep fissures. Not for the first time, Kara, the oldest child, ran away from home, and she began experimenting with drugs. Teddy, the middle child, was still far from a full recovery.

Patrick, the youngest, suffered from life-threatening attacks of asthma. Doctors put him on heavy doses of cortisone and ordered him to stay within a short driving distance of the nearest hospital emergency room.[2]

Meanwhile, Joan took the first important step toward admitting that she was powerless over alcohol. She checked herself into Silver Hill Hospital in New Canaan, Connecticut, where Jackie's late father, Black Jack Bouvier, had frequently gone to dry out. However, Joan's treatments at Silver Hill were not effective, and she then spent some time at a rehab in San Juan Capistrano, California.

When the media got wind of Joan's ordeal, they turned it into a soap opera. Her photo was on the front page of the tabloids when she fell off the wagon and was arrested for drunk driving. She became, in the words of Marcia Chellis, her personal assistant, "the butt of countless jokes inside the Beltway."

"What happens to the human spirit is like what happens to a high cliff when the waves are too strong and too high and too constant," said Muffy Brandon, one of Joan's best friends. "The cliff erodes and the underpinnings get shaky. That's what happened to Joan."

IN AUGUST 1974, faced with certain impeachment, Richard Nixon resigned from office, and Vice President Gerald Ford succeeded him as president. A month later, the early polls showed that Ted Kennedy led all the likely Democratic and Republican candidates for president in 1976.

Ted felt that 1976 was his year. He was confident that he could beat Gerry Ford. But Ted was also worried about what the pressures of a presidential campaign would do to his family. Several of his nephews, for whom he had assumed responsibility after Bobby's death, were in trouble with drugs. Bobby Jr. was arrested for possession of marijuana; he fled to the Berkeley campus in California, where he was spotted living on the street and begging for handouts. And Bobby Jr.'s brother David was seriously addicted to cocaine and heroin.

Closer to home, Ted's children were having nightmares about his running for president; they feared he would be shot dead like their uncles Jack and Bobby. Ted took to telephoning Teddy Jr. every day just so the boy could hear his reassuring voice.

"Do you think Teddy is strong enough?" Ted asked his aides, knowing that the answer was no. He had even greater reservations about Joan's ability to withstand the pressures of a campaign.

"By sheer coincidence," recalled John Lindsay of *Newsweek*, "I was on an airplane with Joan. She had been in a drying-out tank in Point David, which was just four or five miles up the coast from San Clemente [California]. She was coming back and was in a really awful condition. Whatever she'd been out there to have done had not been done. She was vague and she was on tranquilizers. We got down to Dulles terminal that Saturday night. It was raining and miserable. All the kids were there. But Ted wasn't. I went home and said to my wife, 'If this guy takes this family through a presidential campaign, there is no pain in hell that is enough for him.' "

In September 1974, while he still enjoyed a comfortable lead in the polls, Ted Kennedy announced that he would not be a candidate for president in 1976. He cited family responsibilities. When he heard the news, *Newsweek*'s John Lindsay said: "This is the best thing this man has ever done in his life, as a human being."

IF TED'S DECISION not to run for president in 1976 was a test of character, he passed it with flying colors. By taking himself out of the race, however, he had all but handed the White House to Jimmy Carter, a peanut farmer and former governor of Georgia who came from the conservative wing of the Democratic Party, which Ted held in low esteem.

One night in July 1976, during the presidential campaign between Carter and Gerald Ford, Ted went to his brother-in-law Steve Smith's Manhattan apartment for dinner. There, he had a long talk with the historian Arthur Schlesinger Jr., who had been close to his brother Jack.

"I don't want to appear a bad sport," Ted told Schlesinger. "My brothers and I have always played by the rules. I can't change on that. But a lot of people have put a lot of work and belief in things. I can't go to them and say they must trust Carter or that he believes in the things they believe in. I don't know what he believes in myself."

"He was speaking, as he often does, in a rush of words and somewhat cryptically," Schlesinger noted in his diary that night. "He has the Kennedy habit of articulating enough of a sentence to open up a point and then, assuming the point is made, jumping to the next sentence. So I am not altogether clear whether he was talking about Carter in general or in particular relation to national health insurance.

"There was a certain sadness about Ted," Schlesinger's diary entry continued. "One felt he could not escape the apprehension that history may have passed him by. The highest expectations have been instilled in Ted, and now it looks as if Jimmy Carter, whom no one ever heard of, will be the President for the next eight years. Yet one must never forget the unpredictability of life. And Carter will always have the felt presence of Ted Kennedy on his left."

. . .

. . .

In 1977, joan kennedy's mother, Ginny, died the ghastly death of an alcoholic. Ginny's passing was a terrible blow to Joan, not least because Joan saw it as a prophecy of how she herself might end her days. And so, once again, she vowed to do something about her drinking.

At the age of forty—and after nineteen years of marriage—she packed her bags and left Ted. She moved into a condominium apartment in Boston overlooking the Charles River. She began seeing a psychiatrist and attending meetings of Alcoholics Anonymous.

"I needed space—my own space—and time to see what my needs are, now and for the rest of my life," she explained. "It's sad to say, but I think I had to suffer an awful lot and cause my family and friends a lot of trouble in coming to grips with myself. Now that I've faced the drinking problem, I feel that I can do anything I really want to do."[3]

Breaking away from Ted wasn't easy, Joan confessed. And what made it even harder was the fact that Kara, Teddy Jr., and Patrick all chose to remain at home in McLean with their father.

"Ted and I are so different," Joan said. "He's a super-Dad. I'm not a super-Mom. He's like a Pied Piper with our kids and all the nieces and nephews—everything's exuberance and activity. By comparison I'm quiet—good for times when the kids like to cuddle up and just visit. . . ."

Joan enrolled in Lesley College, a small teacher's college in Cambridge, to pursue a master's degree in music education. She and Ted spoke on the phone practically every day, and he frequently made the trip to Boston, where he sometimes participated in Joan's psychiatric sessions.

"People ask whether the newspaper stories about Ted and girls hurt my feelings," Joan said. "Of course they hurt my feelings. They went to the core of my self-esteem. When one grows up feeling that maybe one is sort of special and hoping that one's husband thinks so, and then suddenly, thinking maybe he doesn't. . . . Well, I didn't lose my self-esteem altogether, but it was difficult to hear all the rumors. And I began thinking, well, maybe I'm just not attractive enough or attractive anymore, or whatever, and it was awfully easy to then say, Well, after all, you know, if that's the way it is, I might as well have a drink."[4]

15

————

IN THE MONTHS after Joan left him, Ted Kennedy fell into a brown study. Members of his staff wondered what was bothering him. Was it the public humiliation of being dumped by his wife? After all, it was the senator who usually discarded women like tissue paper, not the other way around. Was it the embarrassment caused by Joan's magazine interviews, in which she divulged intimate details of their marriage? Members of the Kennedy clan were supposed to be bound by the code of *omertà*. Or did it have nothing to do with his personal life? Was it the frustration of seeing his chief Democratic rival, Jimmy Carter, sitting where Ted thought *he* should be sitting—in the Oval Office?

Ted Kennedy and Jimmy Carter were as different as night and day. For starters, Kennedy loved politics and Carter didn't. Kennedy regarded Carter as a pompous, sanctimonious ass, and as the *Times'* Adam Clymer pointed out, "Carter looked down on Kennedy, morally, because of Chappaquiddick. . . . [H]e called Kennedy 'a woman killer.' "[1]

After Carter was inaugurated as president in January 1977, he made a point of not inviting Ted to White House dinners and other official functions. Both in person and through proxies, Carter and Kennedy clashed over their opposing political points of view; Carter preached a brand of fiscal restraint and budget discipline that was a clear rebuke to Kennedy-style liberalism.

By the summer of 1978, the two men were at loggerheads over a number of policy issues, both domestic and foreign. "You talk to Carter," Arthur Schlesinger Jr. said to Ted Kennedy. "Where does he really stand on things? He gives the impression of a man without a center. Is there a center?"

To which Ted replied: "That's the question."[2]

Their sharpest area of disagreement was over Ted's signature issue, national health care. On July 27, 1978, Carter noted in his diary:

> I talked to Kennedy at length this afternoon, and then to Stu [Eizenstat, the president's chief domestic policy adviser] about the health program. Kennedy insists that it be sent up before the [off-year congressional] election. I insist that it not be sent up before the election. . . . [3]

To most Washington observers, it seemed only a matter of time before Ted Kennedy and Jimmy Carter would have the political equivalent of the gunfight at the O.K. Corral. And Carter and his closest political adviser, Chief of Staff Hamilton Jordan, began preparing for just such a showdown.

"People said [about Kennedy's taking on Carter], 'Well, if you had done this and if you had done that, on health care'—and I always said no—you know, Kennedy looked at the polls and saw

Carter was vulnerable," said Ham Jordan. "[Kennedy] wanted to be president and he ran. . . . And that wouldn't have been changed by Carter's calling him more or having him over for dinner, or whatever. I mean, I just, I never, I never bought that."[4]

It wasn't only Ted Kennedy who was looking at the polls. Inflation, interest rates, and unemployment were going through the roof, and more and more people began to wonder whether Carter was up to the job of being president. By the summer of 1978, Carter's poll numbers had plummeted from a 75 percent approval rating to 40 percent. Among Democrats, he was more unpopular than Harry Truman had been in 1952 and Lyndon Johnson in 1968.

As for Carter, he thought his problem was Ted Kennedy. His deep distrust of Ted Kennedy was reflected in his daily diary entries. On July 28, 1978, the president wrote:

> I met again with Kennedy. Outlined what our position was on [the health program]. Told him I needed his support. That if he had to disagree or criticize to go ahead and do it. And I instructed [Joseph] Califano [secretary of health, education, and welfare] to have his press conference tomorrow about noon.[5]

The next entry in Carter's diary read:

> Kennedy had a press conference at 3:00 to blast us on the health care system. I thought he betrayed my trust because he specifically asked us to delay our press conference from Friday noon until later so he could study it more. And then without letting us know, he scheduled his own.[6]

. . .

. . .

As EARLY AS September 1978—more than two years before the 1980 presidential election—Carter's aides began warning him of an almost certain primary challenge by Ted Kennedy. On September 28, Hubert "Herky" Harris, assistant director of the Office of Management and Budget, sent Carter's chief of staff, Hamilton Jordan, a handwritten note:

> I understand [Kennedy] people held meetings in Boston this weekend regarding the campaign. . . . The meetings were to discuss the alternative courses open to Kennedy depending on what *you* representing the President might do. Best I can tell it was a strategy/tactics session, discussing various best case–worst case scenarios, and how Kennedy's campaign could best react. The questions were posed "If I were Ham Jordan, and 'such & such' occurred, what would I do? How would I respond? Etc."
>
> My source is reliable, but this report is for info only. I don't know of any decisions made or specific conclusions drawn. They are clearly *planning*.[7]

On December 9, 1978, Herky Harris's warning seemed to be borne out when Ted Kennedy delivered a speech to an overflow crowd in Memphis, Tennessee, that was widely interpreted as his opening shot for the 1980 Democratic nomination against a sitting president of his own party. Ted did not try to disguise his anger over Carter's plan to increase the military budget and cut back social spending.

"Sometimes a party must sail against the wind," Ted said. "We cannot afford to drift or lie at anchor. We cannot heed the call of those who say it is time to furl the sail."

The audience went wild. But two men standing in the back of the auditorium—Hamilton Jordan and Pat Caddell, President Carter's pollster—did not join in the cheering. When Ted's speech was over, Jordan turned to Caddell and said, "That's it. He's running."[8]

But Ted hadn't quite made up his mind yet. In March 1979, shortly after he celebrated his forty-seventh birthday, Ted visited Carter in the White House. Ted's weight, his flyaway hair, and his Benjamin Franklin–style reading glasses made him look as old as Carter, who was eight years Ted's senior. Carter greeted Ted with a tight, condescending smile, and the two men retired behind closed doors to discuss the knotty issue of national health care. When they were finished, Ted looked at Carter and told him that he had "tentatively" decided to support him for reelection in 1980.

Carter didn't believe him. Nor, for that matter, did anyone else in Washington. In June 1979, the subject of a potential Carter-Kennedy face-off came up at a White House dinner for members of the House of Representatives.

"We are having a good time with the president," recalled Congressman Tom Downey of New York, "and [Carter] comes and joins us. . . . And the conversation turned to the primaries, and Toby [Moffett, a congressman from Connecticut] asked about the Kennedy campaign. And Carter turned to him and said, 'If Ted Kennedy runs in [the] New Hampshire [primary], I'll whip his ass.' "

AND SO, BY the early summer of 1979, Jimmy Carter was poised for an all-out war against Ted Kennedy. But Carter wasn't prepared for what happened next. In the wake of the Islamic revolution in Iran, which toppled the shah and installed the radical Ayatollah Khomeini, the price of crude oil doubled, the supply of oil fell, and long lines of cars began appearing at gas stations all across America.

The energy crisis of 1979 exacerbated the widespread feeling that the country was adrift under Jimmy Carter. All the opinion polls confirmed that impression; they showed that Democrats now preferred Ted Kennedy over Jimmy Carter by a margin of 53 percent to 16 percent.

Carter's presidency appeared to be in a free fall. To save it, he went on television to deliver a fireside chat to the nation. He wore a cardigan to illustrate the need for energy conservation, but the baggy, ill-fitting sweater only made him look like a wimp.

"In a nation that was proud of hard work, strong families, close-knit communities, and our faith in God," he said, "too many of us now tend to worship self-indulgence and consumption."

The president sounded as though he was blaming the American people for the country's problems, instead of assuming responsibility himself. And although he never used the word, his talk became known derisively as Carter's "malaise" speech.

"That speech was so contrary to everything I believe in that it upset me," Ted Kennedy said later. "I was alone watching it. I didn't talk to any political reporters for three weeks before; you know how political reporters are—they keep coming around to take your pulse. . . . [Then] I spent four weeks making a *personal* decision, not even talking with key people you respect."

To make that personal decision, Ted had to take into account his frayed marriage to Joan. Was their relationship repairable? Was it possible for Joan to forget the past and join him in the greatest adventure of their life—the pursuit of the presidency? If he won the White House, could Joan function as First Lady?

To find out the answers to those questions, Ted asked Lawrence Horowitz, a thirty-four-year-old physician and top staffer on Ted's health subcommittee, to convene a panel of experts from around the country to review Joan Kennedy's medical history. Ted wanted to know whether his running for president would put an unbearable strain on Joan's health. For by now it had become clear that Joan had problems that went beyond alcoholism; she was having episodes of severe mood swings that are experienced by people with bipolar disorder.

The daylong meeting took place in the first week of September 1979 at a hotel in Virginia, and it included Joan's principal psychiatrist. When Ted showed up in the evening, the doctors gave him their consensus opinion: To the extent that Joan would be kept busy in a focused and structured atmosphere, a presidential campaign would be a plus, not a minus, because it would relieve Joan of her current feeling of isolation.

Ted also asked Dr. Horowitz to speak with Kara and Teddy Jr. and tell them that their father was seriously considering running for president. (Patrick was already on board and didn't have to be persuaded.)

"And I would say [Kara and Teddy Jr.] were not wildly enthusiastic," Horowitz recalled. "But they . . . didn't say, 'We don't want him to run.' Both of them said, 'If this is what he wants to do, we'll support him.' And out of that and listening to their concerns, I got the senator's permission to go to the White House to ask for Secret Service protection."[9]

Since the days of Joe Kennedy, the Kennedys had been regarded as masters at manipulating the media. Reporters fawned over John and Robert Kennedy when they ran for president. And Ted likewise had many friends in the press. For the rollout of his presidential campaign, Ted offered to give an interview to Roger Mudd of CBS News, who was considered a friend of the family. Ted had helped find a job for Mudd's son, and Mudd had been a guest at Ted's home on Squaw Island.

Mudd and the executives at CBS News jumped at the chance to get Ted in front of the cameras. They agreed to tape two interviews—one at Ted's home on Squaw Island, the other in his Senate office—then splice them together and run the whole thing as an hour-long special in early November—three days before Ted's official announcement that he was running for president.

Ted knew that the CBS brass considered him a big "get"; by giving CBS an exclusive, he was doing the network a favor. He therefore viewed the arrangement with Mudd in the same vein as a political deal—one hand washing the other. In return for doing a softball interview, Mudd would get a leg up in his competition with Dan Rather over who would succeed Walter Cronkite as anchor of the *CBS Evening News.* That, at least, was Ted's theory. In practice, things didn't work out that way when the TV cameras began rolling.

"So he comes across, as so many reporters and journalists in Washington knew him to be, as a physically dominating, very fine-looking, handsome sort of an Irish sculpted lord," Mudd recalled of the interview. "But at times hopelessly inarticulate . . . grasping for words. Not terribly well collected. But nonetheless a major force that just fills the screen. And then suddenly to have this great face and visage not being able to put a complete sentence together in answer to some very simple questions."[10]

"Why do you want to be president?" Mudd asked in the interview.

"Well," Kennedy began, "I'm—were I to—to make the—announcement . . . is because I have a great belief in this country, that it is—has more natural resources than any nation in the world . . . the greatest technology of any country in the world . . . the greatest political system in the world . . . And the energies and the resource-fulness of this nation, I think, should be focused on these prob-lems in a way that brings a sense of restoration in this country by its people . . . And I would basically feel that—that it's imperative for this country to either move forward, that it can't stand still, or other-wise it moves back."

Ted's disastrous performance in the Mudd interview reflected a fatal flaw at the heart of the Kennedy campaign organization: Ted's handlers didn't treat him like an ordinary political candidate who needed to be prepped for his media close-up. Instead, they treated him like royalty. Certain words were never to be mentioned in Ted's presence, words such as "Chappaquiddick" or "alcoholism" or "adultery." Nobody had the guts to speak frankly to Ted about Joan's drinking, Ted's womanizing, and the residual fallout from Chappaquiddick. If these negatives were brought up at all, they were bundled together in a single, innocuous phrase: "the character issue." The only person who was close enough to Ted to force him to confront "the character issue" was Steve Smith, the campaign manager, but according to Susan Estrich, the deputy campaign man-ager, Smith was a total washout.

"He was invisible," said Estrich. "[Steve] disappeared from the campaign. I mean that campaign was just a nightmare . . . at the top. I mean—Steve Smith . . . I recall went to Madrid or something for some extensive period of time during that time."[11]

As a result, said Peter Hart, Ted's chief pollster, "there was no sense of central leadership. . . . I don't think that I was ever asked or given the opportunity to really explore [Chappaquiddick]. . . . I don't think I ever did a focus group for Senator Kennedy, and I'm not sure that there was ever a focus group done in that campaign."[12]

An even bigger problem was the candidate himself. Ted Ken-nedy had always been ambivalent about the presidency. Amateur psychologists speculated that Ted was torn by the idea of leaping over the Kennedy family hierarchy, superseding his dead brothers, and perhaps even succeeding where they had faltered and failed.

There was also a far simpler explanation. "My view," said CBS's Roger Mudd, "is that he wasn't prepared, because he had never really sat down and asked himself [the] question: Why do I, Edward Moore Kennedy, want to run this country? Who are my enemies, who are my friends? Who am I going to reward? Who am I going to punish? He'd never been up to the top of the mountain. And I think he'd never asked himself that question. Simply because he, I suspect . . . could sort of ascend to the nomination and he didn't have to go through that rigorous self-examination that [other politicians] went through and they all are supposed to go through."[13]

Everything that followed the Mudd interview was anticlimactic. On November 4, 1979, Ted's announcement of his candidacy was buried by the news that Iranian students had taken over the United States embassy in Tehran and held fifty-two American diplomats hostage. The sudden upsurge in patriotism and support for President Carter was largely responsible for Ted's defeat in the Iowa caucuses and the New Hampshire primary. The hostage crisis would last for 444 days and color the entire primary campaign. On March 11, 1980, Carter annihilated Ted in the Florida primary, 60.7 percent to 23.2 percent.

Later that month, Jackie Kennedy Onassis convened a group of friends in her New York apartment to discuss how Ted could gracefully bow out of the contest. But then, suddenly, Ted won two primaries in a row—in New York and Pennsylvania. "We were always looking for a clean opportunity to get out," a member of the Kennedy inner circle told the writer Theodore H. White. "We said if we lost in New York, we could get out; if we lost in Pennsylvania, we could get out. But we won in both, so we couldn't get out."

Those victories only prolonged the agony. For although Ted won the last batch of primaries in June, Carter's lead in the delegate count had become insurmountable. On June 5, 1980, Frank Moore and Bill Cable, who handled congressional liaison for President Carter, sent a "confidential" memo to Chief of Staff Hamilton Jordan:

About 11:40 A.M. Senator Kennedy talked to the Speaker [Tip O'Neill]. After his phone call the Speaker called Bill Cable and told him the following. The President should not push hard with Kennedy at their meeting this afternoon—he should not be confrontational. The Senator is pleased that his victories on Tuesday gave him a dignified way out and raised his stature within the Senate and within the Democratic constituencies. . . . According to the Speaker, "Ted sounds like a changed man—very relieved."

HE *WAS* A changed man. The gut-wrenching experience of the primary campaign had changed him. But not in the way Speaker O'Neill meant.

At the start of the campaign, when the Carter administration seemed at a total loss over how to cope with long gas lines, runaway inflation, and the Iranian revolution, everyone told Ted Kennedy that he was a shoo-in for the nomination. And he believed them—first, because he wanted to, and second, because it bolstered his belief in the legend of Kennedy invincibility.

"And he sort of then started to look at the race in a tactical manner," said Ted's pollster, Peter Hart. "And as he looked at it in a tactical manner he lost the strategic advantage that he really had. His voice. Which was his strength. And his voice was his vision. . . . I would tell you that Edward Kennedy lost his way during that period of time. . . . And it wasn't until he had lost the nomination that he got back the fundamentals. That was the ultimate irony of the election. He found his [liberal] voice."[14]

Susan Estrich, the deputy campaign manager, witnessed first-hand how Ted evolved during the campaign. "I have a very positive view of that [campaign] and what happened," she said, "and the evolution of attitudes toward women, and toward abortion and a whole range of issues. . . . The 1980 [Democratic Party] platform was the first time that sexual orientation ever appeared in a party platform. And it was because of . . . Ted."[15]

Ted had become the tribune not only of the sick and poor and helpless but also of women and gays and lesbians. Ted's speech at the 1980 Democratic National Convention ranked with the great convention speeches of the past—William Jennings Bryan's "cross of gold" speech in 1896; Hubert Humphrey's "bright sunshine of human rights" speech in 1948; and Adlai Stevenson's "talk sense to the American people" speech in 1952.

"I congratulate President Carter on his victory here," Ted said. ". . . And someday, long after this convention, long after the signs come down and the crowds stop cheering, and the bands stop playing, may it be said of our campaign that we kept the faith. May it be said of our Party in 1980 that we found our faith again. . . . For me, a few hours ago, this campaign came to an end. For all those whose cares have been our concern, the work goes on, the cause endures, the hope still lives, and the dream shall never die."[16]

PART FOUR

"Victory out of Failure"

16

———

AFTER THE DEMOCRATIC Convention, Ted and Joan flew to the Cape, and there, in their gray-shingled home on Squaw Island overlooking Hall's Creek, Joan brought up the subject of divorce.

"I remember Ted saying to me . . . 'You're doing so great, Joansie, how about moving back to Washington, to McLean?' He didn't say, 'I love you' or 'I want you to come back' or 'I'm going to be good.' . . . But I sort of knew that he would never make any changes.

"And I guess I just decided that I felt too good about myself to put up with what—I had been putting up with for some time," Joan continued. "He said, 'I want to stay married to you.' He said I could have all the freedom I wanted. I could carry on with my life. 'You could see anybody you want to see.' How many women are offered that? The money, the prestige, the freedom."[1]

Racked with doubts about her decision, Joan turned for support to her favorite sister-in-law, Jackie Kennedy Onassis.

"I spent four hours talking to Jackie," Joan recalled. "She said she's crazy about Ted, but she's known for years that I should have done it fifteen years ago. She was so supportive. She even suggested I use her New York lawyer. If Jackie recommends him and says he's distinguished, he must be good. Jackie said not to worry about Ted, that he'll be fine. She said I should look out for myself.

"Jackie also told me that she wishes she had given me this advice before and maybe I wouldn't have gotten so sick," Joan continued, referring to her alcoholism. "But back then, fifteen years ago, I probably wouldn't have been able to take her advice."[2]

Even now, it wasn't easy. Joan knew that a divorce from Ted Kennedy would change everything—where she lived, the amount of money she could spend, how people would treat her. If only she were thick-skinned enough to tolerate Ted's philandering. But she wasn't a hardened case like Rose Kennedy, who had taught herself to look the other way whenever her husband strayed. Joan wore her heart on her sleeve, which, ironically, was one of the qualities that had drawn Ted to her in the first place.

Ted did not welcome the circus of publicity that was sure to accompany the announcement of a Kennedy divorce. And yet, he still cared enough for Joan to realize that, at this lamentable stage of their marriage, divorce was probably her best course. However, he asked her for a favor: would Joan postpone the announcement of their decision to divorce until after the inauguration of Jimmy Carter? As a loyal Democrat, Ted was expected to campaign for his old adversary, and he wanted Joan to join him on the hustings. Joan agreed, and for the next couple of months, they appeared as a loving couple at Carter campaign rallies.

After the election was over, Joan was represented at the divorce proceedings by Alexander Folger, the attorney recommended by Jackie Kennedy. Folger's upper-class demeanor led some people to suppose that he abided by the legal equivalent of the Marquess of Queensberry rules. That, however, was not the case; he was as tough as the toughest Massachusetts divorce lawyer. And from the outset, the two sides engaged in a contentious battle over the terms of the financial settlement.

"To determine [Joan's] living allowance, the [Kennedy] lawyers were averaging her expenses of the last four years," her assistant, Marcia Chellis, observed. "Joan felt that the past year was a more realistic one, but Ted's lawyer pointed out that people spend more during a campaign year."[3]

As part of the settlement, Joan wanted Ted to pay for repairs and improvements in her Boston condo and the Squaw Island house. She drew up a list of what needed to be done—everything from painting and slipcovering to remodeling and cabinetwork.

"Ted ignored me [during our marriage]," she told Marcia Chellis. To which Chellis commented: "But that was in the past. . . . In her battles with Ted she may have been both difficult and demanding, but she would no longer be ignored."[4]

Indeed, Joan surprised everyone—perhaps most of all herself—by her resolve and willpower. She was shrewd enough to guess that Ted would be vulnerable just before the start of a reelection campaign, when he was polishing his image in the media. As the election year 1982 approached, the last thing Ted wanted was an angry wife complaining to the media about his adulteries.

"I'm going to stick this out until I get what I want," Joan said. "He thinks I'm too nice to fight, but I'll play my trump card. . . . I'll say, 'He throws millions at the poor, but he's stingy with his wife.'

He wants this over before the Senate election next fall, but I'm in no rush. They are treating me like an alcoholic who is still drinking and I won't let them."[5]

In the settlement, Joan received a lump-sum payment of $5 million, plus child support and annual alimony of $175,000. But Ted was adamant about keeping the Squaw Island home.

"When Ted and I were getting a divorce," Joan said, "he insisted on the house. 'You can go over and get a really nice house in Osterville with all your Republican friends. This is Kennedy territory.' I really took offense [at that remark]. 'Like hell it is. The Bennetts were here in 1901. . . . This is where I'm staying. . . .

"That house means more to me than any other place in the world," she went on. "It's where my children, their friends, and I go from late May until September, and we are there often in the winter months, too. I use the house as a retreat. I go there to be alone to think, read, walk on the beach, play my piano. Just a few days there and I'm renewed."[6]

The frail and delicate Joan Bennett Kennedy wouldn't budge. She was determined to have the deed to ownership of the house transferred to her name. What's more, she insisted on making Ted pay for its upkeep.

In the end, Joan won on both counts.

SHORTLY BEFORE CHRISTMAS in 1985, Ted called Bob Shrum, who had written the famous "the dream shall never die" speech, and asked him to come to Hyannis Port. Speculation was mounting that, after the New Year, Ted would announce his intention to run for the White House in 1988.

"I know, you're not going to run for president," Shrum said, as the two men settled down over their martini glasses in the living room of the Big House.

"That's right," Kennedy said. "And I don't want to argue."

"I'm only going to say one thing," Shrum said. "You get to run against George [Herbert Walker] Bush and that really is your best chance."

"I know that," Kennedy said, "and I don't want to run."[7]

Ted made the formal announcement in a five-minute speech on TV. "I will run for reelection to the Senate," he said. "I know that this decision means that I may never be president. But the pursuit of the presidency is not my life. Public service is. . . . The thing that matters most, the greatest difference we can make, is to speak out, to stand up to lead, and to move this nation forward. For me at this time the right place is the Senate."

H E HAD LIBERATED himself from the long shadow of the presidency—or, as he put it, from "the fog surrounding my political plans."[8] From now on, he wanted to be judged by one thing and one thing only: his performance in the Senate.

"Kennedy is at his best when he is not in the running," wrote Garry Wills. ". . . [T]he reporters following him in 1980 noticed a sense of freedom growing on him as his chances faded. He performed best when he was showing his mettle as a survivor, not bidding to take over. Forced by fame, by his name, toward power, he tightens up. Allowed to back off, he relaxes."[9]

Ted threw himself into his Senate work. In 1985, he and Republican Lowell Weicker mustered the necessary votes to override a veto by President Reagan of legislation to impose economic sanctions on the apartheid government of South Africa. That same year,

Ted and Chris Dodd introduced a bill that granted employees up to twelve weeks of unpaid leave to deal with a family medical crisis.

During the eight conservative years of Ronald Reagan's presidency, Ted remained an unrepentant liberal. He traveled widely to the poorest sections of Appalachia, including the hamlet of Little Mud, Kentucky, where he pledged to be the advocate for the average man and woman, "a voice for the voiceless."

"He is the first Kennedy to be a loser in politics, and he gives every sign of not anticipating a second chance," wrote the columnist Murray Kempton. "He makes witness now, not as a candidate, but as a kind of steward; he travels to call attention not to himself but to the needs of others. . . . Since no tactic can avail him any longer, we have to assume that only principle carried him to Little Mud. His generation of the Kennedys can never command again; it endures in him only to oppose, the most elevated of all political functions. If he lives wherever ghosts may live, John F. Kennedy, the grandest of successes, must be surprised and proud to have a brother who could bring such a victory out of failure."[10]

Despite his profound political differences with Ronald Reagan, Ted maintained a cordial relationship with the president. But in July 1987, when Reagan nominated Judge Robert H. Bork to the U.S. Supreme Court, Ted unleashed a torrent of invective. For those with a short memory, Ted reminded them that it had been Bork, as solicitor general, who had done Richard Nixon's dirty work and fired Archibald Cox as the special Watergate prosecutor.

"Robert Bork's America," Kennedy said, "is a land in which women would be forced into back-alley abortions, blacks would sit at segregated lunch counters, rogue police could break down citizens' doors in midnight raids, schoolchildren could not be taught about evolution, writers and artists could be censored at the whim of government, and the doors of the federal courts would be shut on the fingers of millions of citizens for whom the judiciary is—and often is the only—protector of the individual rights that are at the heart of our democracy."

Ted came in for some well-deserved criticism for painting Bork as a wild-eyed fascist, which was patently unfair to the judge. Bork's conservative supporters accused Ted of indulging in demagoguery, but they never really recovered from Ted's initial salvo. Three months later, and after hundreds of hours of testimony, the Senate rejected Bork's nomination 58–42.

Republicans responded to their defeat at the hands of Ted Kennedy with a mixture of emotions—anger, frustration, bemusement, and grudging respect. "Just think of Kennedy's monumental hypocrisy of defending women by attacking Bork, while Kennedy harassed women all his life," Tony Blankley, the former editorial-page editor of the conservative *Washington Times,* told the author of this book. "On the other hand, Republicans understood that Kennedy was just taking care of business."[11]

Grover Norquist, the conservative grand sachem who founded Americans for Tax Reform in 1985 at the request of President Reagan—and served on the board of directors of the National Rifle Association and the American Conservative Union—expressed admiration for Ted's political skills.

"I've worked with Kennedy on several issues, including the deregulation of railroads and airlines," Norquist told the author of this book. "He had the brilliance to think three steps ahead. I've also worked with him on immigration issues and the goal of bringing Iraq War translators to the United States. We put together a left-right coalition, which included David Kean, chairman of the American Conservative Union; Senator Sam Brownback of Kansas; and Ted Kennedy. Ted was always civil. He always made a point of calling me himself. Recently, I was in Utah and I got a call from

Kennedy telling me that everything was moving ahead. He's pleasant, cheerful, easy to work with."[12]

But ted's metamorphosis was only half complete. When he wasn't accomplishing parliamentary miracles on the floor of the Senate, he was still behaving like a frat boy on a drunken toot. He and his bachelor pal, Senator Chris Dodd, were involved in a couple of sleazy episodes that made news, including the sexual harassment of a waitress at La Brasserie, a well-known restaurant on Capitol Hill.

Following his divorce, Ted moved into the "Big House"—his father's house—in the Kennedy Compound, where his mother still lived. He had always viewed Hyannis Port, not McLean, Virginia, or Washington, D.C., as his true home. On weekends, after the Senate adjourned, he would fly to the Cape with one of his girlfriends. His schedule rarely varied: He and the girl would arrive between 6:00 p.m. and 8:00 p.m. at the Big House, where his private chef, Neil Connolly, had dinner waiting for them. Often they would be joined by friends, usually Senator Chris Dodd or former senator John Varick Tunney, both of whom brought along *their* weekend companions.

Host and guests would unwind with a glass or two of Irish whiskey, and then sit down for a large seafood dinner on the verandah overlooking the ocean. Cordials were passed around after dessert. Sometimes Ted would screen a movie in the Kennedys' private theater.

First thing Saturday morning, Ted would go for a bracing swim in the ocean and then partake of a hearty breakfast of pancakes or crêpes. By 11:00 a.m., Ted and his guests would board his boat, the *Mya*, for a day's sail. Neil Connolly saw to it that the *Mya* was stocked with sandwiches, seafood salad, beer, and cases of red and white wine.

Heavy weather did not deter Ted. His guests might choose to stay on shore, but he would sail, rain or shine, in the winter as well as in the spring and summer, even in stormy weather. He was content to sail alone, and he generally did not return until five o'clock in the afternoon.

On Sunday mornings, he would attend Mass at Our Lady of Victory Church in nearby Centerville. When his mother was still alive, he might bring a priest to the Big House to say Mass for her. After lunch, he boarded a private plane and flew back to Washington.[13]

STORIES ABOUT TED KENNEDY'S abuse of alcohol and his compulsive womanizing became a staple of tabloid journalism. He was romantically linked with many prominent playmates: ski champ Suzie Chaffee, Countess Lana Campbell, socialite Helga Wagner, British debutante Louise Steel, and German princess Angela Wepper.

However, one relationship received scant media attention—his six-year-long love affair with a saucy blonde by the name of Claudia Cummings. Ted went to great lengths to keep Claudia under wraps. Why he did so was anyone's guess. It was possible that he was more smitten with Claudia than he was with any of his other paramours. It was also possible that Claudia, who later became a backup singer for Jimmy Buffett, simply wasn't the type Ted wanted to be publicly associated with.

At the time they met, in early 1986, Claudia—a five-foot-eight-inch, one-hundred-and-fifteen-pound former Miss Alabama—was working as an Eastern Airlines stewardess. Ted ran into her on a flight from West Palm Beach to Washington National Airport, and an affair quickly developed. The normally frugal Ted lavished Claudia with a full-length Blackglama mink coat, flowers, love notes, and promises he wouldn't keep.

"During a trip to Ireland with Claudia in the late eighties," said a source close to the Kennedy family, "Ted took along Teddy Junior more or less to act as a beard for him with Claudia. Ted introduced Claudia as his son Teddy's girlfriend, and even insisted that Claudia make a point of being seen going into Teddy's bedroom at night, then come into his, Ted's, room through a connecting door."

Teddy Jr., who was known to friends for his exceptionally sensitive nature, developed a crush on Claudia. Unlike his younger brother, Patrick, a more thick-skinned sort who had adopted his father's careless attitude toward women, Teddy Jr. didn't have the stomach for womanizing. In March 1992, when Teddy learned that his father had abruptly ended his affair with Claudia, the young man called her and cried his heart out.[14]

By then, ted's self-destructive behavior—his compulsive eating, boozing, and sexual escapades—had developed an unstoppable momentum of its own. The inevitable crack-up occurred on the Friday of Easter weekend in 1991 in Palm Beach, the scene of many past Kennedy revels. Just before midnight, Ted woke up his son Patrick, twenty-three, and his nephew William Kennedy Smith, thirty, and asked them to go bar crawling with him.

Later that night, Smith returned to the Kennedy mansion on North Ocean Avenue with Patricia Bowman, a woman he had picked up at Au Bar. Patricia Bowman later charged that Smith raped her on the lawn of the estate, while Ted (naked except for a long-tailed

Oxford shirt) and Patrick (who was making love to another woman) were within earshot, and did nothing to stop the rape.

In the morning, Ted hid from the police when they showed up at the Kennedy mansion to investigate the rape charges. The police later said they were investigating possible obstruction-of-justice charges against the senator.

Ted was shaken by the public's reaction to the scandal, which was far worse than the political reverberations from Chappaquiddick. Though Ted himself was not charged with the alleged rape, most people held him responsible for leading his young son and nephew into such a sleazy mess. According to a *Boston Herald/ WCVB-TV* poll, 62 percent of Massachusetts voters said they believed that Kennedy should not run for reelection in 1994.

Realizing his predicament, Ted sought the help of one of his closest friends in the Senate, Orrin Hatch, a conservative Mormon from Utah. "Now, Ted [didn't come] here and [say], 'Orrin, will you help me?' " Hatch recalled. "He didn't say it that way. He wouldn't say it that way. He said, 'Orrin, can we send the media out to you?' I said I'd be glad to help, because I didn't think he deserved the pummeling he got on that [Palm Beach] issue. . . .

"Well," Hatch continued, "I believed that to the extent that he can, he really cares for me, and I've been to his home many times, and he's always been gracious and so forth. I do care for him and so I said to him . . . 'Ted, if you keep acting like this, I'm going to send the Mormon missionaries to you.' "

"His old Irish face got all red and his eyes kind of teared up and he said, 'I'm just about ready for them.' "[15]

17

THE POLITICAL LEGACY that Ted had built over the years in Massachusetts seemed to be falling apart," recalled a Kennedy family lawyer. "He was close to being suicidal. He was slowly killing himself each day; drinking himself to death, not eating right, not taking care of himself at all. He wandered around Hyannis Port half drunk, unshaven, looking like a bum. He would stop people and start inane conversations. He'd stop children and talk to them. It appeared that he was losing it. His nephews and sons were always rounding him up."[1]

He held court at Baxter's Fish 'n Chips and Boathouse Club, a local hangout, where he'd sing along with Carroll Hill, the longtime piano player, and hit on attractive tourists.

"He'd get to-go fried fish or shrimp and chips and eat on a bench behind the restaurant, all by himself," said the bartender. "He was really obese, and he'd have a cap pulled down over his face so that he wouldn't be recognized by anybody who knew him, or let it get to the gossip pages that he was stuffing himself."[2]

AND THEN, SUDDENLY, he came to himself. Dire circumstances demanded dire remedies, and with his career in the Senate hanging in the balance, he made a decision that put the Kennedy legacy on the line. He announced that he was going to address the torrent of criticism over his part in the Palm Beach rape scandal by delivering a speech at Harvard's John F. Kennedy School of Government.

On October 15, 1991, a warm, gusty fall afternoon, a grim-faced Ted Kennedy stood before a mixed audience of students, academics, and the media and proceeded to make amends to the voters of Massachusetts, who held his fate in their hands. It was the week before jury selection was to begin in William Kennedy Smith's rape trial, and it was an amazing moment in American history—nothing quite like it had ever happened before.

Ted freely admitted to the "disappointment of friends and many others who rely on me to fight the good fight. To them I say: I recognize my own shortcomings—the faults in the conduct of my private life. . . . I believe that each of us as individuals must not only struggle to make a better world but to make ourselves better, too."

Afterward, Kennedy spokesman Paul Donovan told reporters: "He knew people had concerns, and he felt it best to address these concerns. He felt he owed it to the people of Massachusetts."

But Donovan and others in Ted Kennedy's brain trust knew that words alone would not suffice. If Ted was going to win reelection against his expected Republican opponent—a telegenic, well-funded businessman by the name of Mitt Romney—Ted needed a fundamental overhaul of his image. He was about to turn sixty years old, and he had to put his skirt chasing behind him once and for all. Most important, he had to settle down with a wife. The odds of reeling Joan back in were slim to none. Nor would any of Ted's other women, such as his longtime lover Palm Beach socialite Dragana Lickle, fit the bill.[3]

In this bleak season for the fading Kennedy Dynasty, Ted turned to the woman who had helped him write his mea culpa speech at Harvard—Victoria Reggie. An attractive thirty-seven-year-old, recently divorced mother of two, Vicki was a corporate lawyer in Washington. Unlike Joan, she was a fiercely independent woman, who had been called "a bold personality, strong-minded and direct." She was more than a match for Ted.

Vicki grew up in Crowley, Louisiana (population 17,000), and was a graduate of New Orleans's Tulane University and a summa cum laude from Tulane Law School, where she was editor of the *Law Review*. She and her former husband, Grier Raclin, a telecommunications lawyer, had two children, Curran, eight, and Caroline, six.

"She was definitely looking for someone different from Grier," said Karen Kilgore, one of Vickie's Tulane sorority sisters. "Ted is handsome and successful and outgoing like her. Grier is a little quieter."

Vicki's family, which was of Lebanese Catholic descent, had ties to the Kennedys going back more than thirty years. Vicki's father, Edmund Reggie, a retired judge, had run the 1960 presidential campaign of John F. Kennedy in the state of Louisiana. He had also run Bobby's and Ted's primary campaigns in the state. Unfortunately, Judge Reggie was currently under federal indictment on eleven counts of bank fraud for his part in the 1986 collapse of a savings and loan. But at this point, the Kennedy people doubtless shrugged, "Nobody's perfect."

Vicki and Ted had begun dating in June 1991. By the following October, she was seated in the front row of the Palm Beach courtroom, listening to Ted reply to questions from the witness stand in the William Kennedy Smith rape trial. Vicki had coached Ted on his testimony, and from time to time, he'd look over and smile at her, and she would smile back.[4]

They were married on July 3, 1992, in a civil ceremony at Ted's home in McLean, Virginia.* On the eve of the wedding, Vicki's sister, Alicia Freysinger, said: "My sister will be a Kennedy; that's not a scary thing. I know who he is. She knows who he is."

THE MARRIAGE WAS a good fit. Friends said that Ted gave his word to Vicki that he would cut back on his drinking and stop seeing other women, and that Vicki said, half in jest, "If you don't, I'll cut your throat with a rusty razor."

"Ted and Vicki have serious quarrels like any other married couple," said a longtime Kennedy friend, "but they also have a lot of fun together. She likes a drink as much as he does, and drinking together is one of their favorite things to do. They drink, joke, laugh, and tell stories together. From the start, Vicki was one of the boys. She likes a ribald joke, and can tell them as well.

"Ted has always been extremely interested in women until he gets sexually satisfied, then he wants to be with the guys," the friend continued. "Vicki's one of the first women who was different, and certainly that's one of the reasons he married her.

---

*Two years later, the Catholic Church granted Ted an annulment of his marriage to Joan, declaring that marriage to be null and void. Joan did not contest the annulment decree; she agreed that Ted had never intended to honor his marriage vow to be faithful.

"Vicki also has a sense of the theatrical that Teddy likes. For staff office parties, Ted and Vicki have an affinity for costumes and mini-plays that are often inside-the-Beltway satire. One Christmas, he painted his face green, dyed his hair lime, and donned a Santa suit. The theme was 'How the Gingrich stole the election.' Vicki came as Shirley Temple wearing butterfly wings. Another time, Ted dressed as a dinosaur that he named 'Tyrannosaurus Sex.' "

Friends described Vicki as the consummate political animal. "She instinctively looks out for him," said one. "For example, when they are having a drink in a public place, and she spots a camera aimed their way, she will move Ted's drink out of sight or stand in front of it.[5]

"Vicki also has a sharp sense of the importance of Ted's political legacy. It was at Vicki's insistence that provisions were made to add a wing to the John F. Kennedy Library in Boston to house Ted's papers, memorabilia from his life and career, and eventually to serve as a shrine to his accomplishments."[6]

FROM THE BEGINNING, all three of Ted's children were opposed to the marriage, and they let their father know how they felt. They were understandably concerned about their inheritance. How much of their father's fortune, estimated at more than $30 million, would come to them? There was a very real likelihood that the bulk of their father's estate would go to Vicki and, by extension, to Vicki's children, Curran and Caroline.

"When Vicki and Ted were talking marriage, the last thing he had on his mind was a premarital legal contract," said a Kennedy family lawyer. "His lawyers begged him to get a prenup. Everybody advised him to do it. But he didn't. His kids are furious because Vicki is going to get everything.

"He has left trusts for his children," this attorney continued. "That was handled many years ago. But they aren't going to divide his estate. That will be Vicki's to do with as she pleases.

"The kids never minded their father's relationships with women. They always accepted it as part of his character. They know it's something of a tradition in their family. But the idea of sharing their fortune with another family was appalling.

"The one thing Vicki and her kids will not get is the Hyannis Port house. The day Ted passes away, she must move out. Ted's desire is that the house be turned over to the JFK Library to be preserved as a museum. The exact terms will have to be worked out because the neighbors are appalled at the idea of tourists trooping through the streets of Hyannis Port. It's bad enough that in summer there is a stream of cars driving through to get a look. So that will have to be worked out. One thought was that it only be open in wintertime."[7]

FRIENDS AND MEMBERS of Ted's family, who were accustomed to the old way of doing things at Hyannis Port, were less than thrilled by the changes that Vicki brought with her. And they tended to describe Vicki's new broom in melodramatic terms.

"Until Vicki came on the scene, Kara, Teddy, and Patrick had the run of the place," said a family insider. "But as soon as Vicki moved in, everything changed. One of the first things she did was to erect NO TRESPASSING signs on the beach. For as long as anyone in Hyannis Port could remember, the Kennedys had always allowed their neighbors to walk across the beach to get to the water, or just as a short cut.

"The next thing was telling the kids that she expected plenty of notice before they showed up at the Big House. Vicki was upset to discover that Kara, Teddy, and Patrick raided the pantry and refrigerators. So she had locks installed. The kids were expected to help shop and bring some of their own food.

"As you can imagine, all of this led to open warfare between Vicki and the Kennedy kids, with Ted silently taking Vicki's side. As a result, his relationship with his children was affected. They obviously still love their father, but there is a deep sense of resentment and even betrayal. There's a sense in which pushing them out of their inheritance was the worst sin he could have committed. They think that Vicki and her kids are going to get a lot of what should have stayed in their family."

T ED'S MARRIAGE TO Vicki came as an even bigger shock to Joan than it did to her children. For weeks, she refused to leave her apartment or answer her phone. Though Joan had dated several eligible bachelors during the decade she had been divorced from Ted, none of those relationships had panned out, and she still looked upon Ted as her chief male protector. "Aides in Kennedy's office had standing orders to put her through to him whenever she called," Adam Clymer noted.[8] Joan instinctively turned to Ted whenever her drinking got her into trouble, which it did with increasing frequency.

One time, in 1988, Joan crashed her car into a fence in Centerville on Cape Cod. The judge suspended her license for forty-five days and ordered her to attend an alcohol-education program. Another time, in 1991, a policeman pulled her over on an expressway after he observed her drinking vodka straight from a bottle. Throughout the 1990s, she was in and out of hospitals and rehab centers, but nothing seemed to help.

There was something odd about Joan's struggle with her addiction. People who attend meetings of Alcoholics Anonymous, as Joan did, are encouraged to take personal responsibility for their problems, and to deal with them in private. But Joan seemed to go out of her way to publicize the details of her bumpy journey on the road to sobriety. "It's such a relief to be free [of alcohol]," she would tell reporters. But each interview was followed by another spectacular slip, which also made the pages of the Boston newspapers. It was hard to avoid the suspicion that Joan was seeking attention—or sending out SOS signals for help.

In 1994, in the midst of Ted's bruising reelection campaign against Mitt Romney, Joan sent her attorneys back to court to demand that she be given more money in a revised divorce settlement. Her timing was calculated to generate the maximum amount of press attention, which didn't thrill Ted or his wife of two years, Vicki Kennedy, who was already fed up with Joan's constant intrusions into her married life. Even Ted's children were appalled at their mother's timing, and they convinced her to put the case on hold until after the election.

Ted won the election. But it marked the first time that a Kennedy had received less than 60 percent of the vote in Massachusetts.

From that electoral low, the path of Ted's life could only head upward. Sometime later, former senator and longtime Kennedy friend George Smathers declared, "The combination of age and a new wife is doing the job."[9]

In the 100th Congress (1987–88), Ted achieved an astonishing record. "He shoved thirty-nine bills through his committee and into law, including a big AIDS package and restrictions on the use of lie detectors in the workplace," noted the *Washington Post*. "Of nine Democratic objectives in the Senate for [the] second session of the 101st Congress, five will be routed through Kennedy's Labor Committee."[10]

There were several explanations for Ted's increasing effectiveness as the years went by. To begin with, he did not personalize political differences, and he always showed respect for his ideological adversaries. In the words of the late muckraking journalist Jack Newfield, "Kennedy has found a way to be both bipartisan in his affections and alliances and partisan in his belief that government has an obligation to make America a more equal country."[11]

As a result, Ted had many admirers on the Republican side of the aisle. "Ted always keeps his word," said Senator John McCain. "This is essential in a small group of people like the Senate. There is no bullshit with Ted. You know exactly where he is coming from. He does what he says he will do. He is a great listener in a body of poor listeners. This makes it easy to deal with him. Look, I've had my fights with him. We disagree on a lot of things. But Ted doesn't have a mean bone in his body. He likes people. And he doesn't hold a grudge."[12]

Second, Ted did a lot of favors, big and small. In 1998, Senator Trent Lott, then the Republican leader of the Senate, sent Ted a handwritten note, which Ted framed and hung in his office. "Your thoughtfulness truly amazes me," Lott wrote. "First the print from Cape Cod. Then the special edition of *Profiles in Courage*. I brought it home and reread it. What an inspiration! Thank you, my friend, for your many courtesies. If the world only knew."[13]

Late one night, Orrin Hatch, the conservative Republican from Utah, came upon Ted in the Capitol after Ted was already three sheets to the wind.

"Ted," Hatch said, "I've got a favor to ask."

"Done!" Ted said, throwing his arm around Hatch.

"No, hear me out," Hatch said. "You remember my aide, Frank Madsen. . . ."

"Great fellow! Great fellow!"

"He's now in Boston. . . ."

"My hometown! My hometown!"

Hatch then asked his favor: Would Ted join him in speaking to two hundred young Mormon missionaries at Boston's Faneuil Hall? Ted instantly agreed, and Hatch had his office draw up a memo. The next day, Ted called Hatch.

"Orrin," he said, "what else did I agree to?"

Several weeks later, Ted Kennedy stood in front of an audience of young Mormons in Faneuil Hall. He had kept his promise.[14]

YET ANOTHER IMPORTANT key to Ted's success as a senator was his staff, which numbered more than one hundred, and was by far the largest on Capitol Hill. Like his father and his brother Jack before him, Ted hired the best and brightest assistants, even if he had to pay some of them out of his own pocket.

"Other Senate offices aspire to run the same kind of political operation, but they don't have the same Prussian precision that Kennedy's staff does," remarked an aide who had worked for three senators.[15]

"Kennedy uses staff people the way Pony Express riders used horses: Ride 'em hard and then leap to another horse," said Thomas M. Rollins, former staff director of Kennedy's Labor Committee. "He's a genius at managing people."[16]

Ted was known for his ability to absorb a prodigious amount of information in a short period of time. When he left the office at the end of the day, he was always accompanied by "The Bag," which contained his homework for the evening. "Material is sorted into four folders: Must Do, which includes staff memos—usually one page, single-spaced—on the following day's activities; Invitations; Signature Needed; selected Mail and Other Reading," wrote the *Washington Post*'s Rick Atkinson. "In the morning, Kennedy hands The Bag to a secretary, who parcels out memos and other documents to the appropriate staffers. Scribbled in the margins are the senator's notations and marching orders, usually terse and barely legible: 'see me' or 'let's talk' or 'o.k.' or, if something displeases him, 'ugh!' "[17]

Ambassador Joseph Kennedy with wife Rose and (from left) Kathleen, Ted, Patricia, Jean, and Robert in London, c. 1938. Ted grew up idolizing his father and never seriously challenged his preeminence. (HULTON-DEUTSCH COLLECTION/CORBIS)

Back row, from left: Kathleen, Joe Jr., Patricia, Rose, and Ted. Middle row: John, Eunice, Joseph, and Jean. Front: Robert and Rosemary. The children were pitted against one another in contests of strength and skill.

(ULLSTEIN BILD/THE GRANGER COLLECTION, NEW YORK)

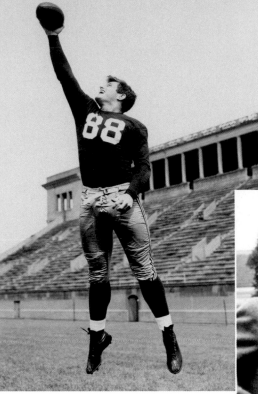

In the 1955 Harvard-Yale football game, Ted caught Harvard's only touchdown pass. His prowess on the field earned Jack's praise and envy.
(AP IMAGES)

Jack, Bobby, and Teddy, 1960. After Jack's assassination, Ted and Bobby embraced the mythic JFK who was lionized as a revolutionary cultural figure. (PHOTOFEST)

Newlyweds Ted and Joan Kennedy, 1958. "I had to clean, cook, do the laundry, and I really learned a lot," Joan said. *"It was fun—for a while!"*
(PHILIPPE HALSMAN/MAGNUM PHOTOS)

Right: Newly elected Senator Edward Kennedy, 1962. As the youngest of nine children, Ted found it natural to defer to his elders, an essential trait in the Senate. (JOHN LOENGARD/ TIME LIFE PICTURES/GETTY IMAGES)

Below: Bobby and Ted flank Jackie at JFK's funeral, November 25, 1963. Ted believed Jack had been martyred because of his efforts to unlatch the door of opportunity for millions of Americans. (AP IMAGES)

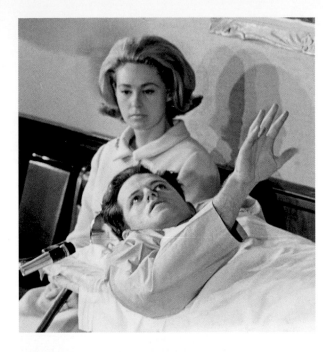

Joan comforts Ted after his near-fatal plane crash in 1964. Following his recovery, Ted was greeted on the floor of the Senate as a conquering hero. (BOSTON HERALD)

Ted Kennedy eulogizing his brother Robert at St. Patrick's Cathedral in 1968. He was truly alone—the last surviving son of his father's dynastic schemes, the last surviving father of his brothers' children. (GEORGE TAMES/NEW YORK TIMES/REDUX)

Senator Kennedy's car after it was fished out of Poucha Pond on Chappaquiddick, July 1969. "There's been a terrible accident," Ted said. "The car's gone off the bridge down by the beach, and Mary Jo is in it." (BETTMANN/CORBIS)

Ted tries to elude photographers after reporting the fatal accident to the police. "I was overcome . . . by a jumble of emotions—grief, fear, doubt, exhaustion, panic, confusion and shock," he said. (CORBIS)

Above: Ted shakes hands with President Nixon at a White House ceremony in 1970. For as long as anyone in Washington could remember, Nixon had been obsessed with the Kennedys. (CORBIS)

Left: Joan and Ted escort their son from the hospital after his right leg was amputated in 1973. "Sometimes I hear Teddy Jr. crying," Ted said. "We try to make out as though we have not noticed his sadness, but it tears the heart out of me." (BETTMANN/CORBIS)

Ted with his mother in an undated photograph. As Ted grew up, Rose began to favor him, the son most like her father. (PHOTOFEST)

CBS correspondent Roger Mudd questions Ted on his 1980 presidential bid. He was not "able to put a complete sentence together in answer to some very simple questions," Mudd said. (CBS/LANDOV)

Senators Kennedy and Hillary Clinton in 2007. Ted was leery of the Clintons' efforts to distance themselves from the liberal Kennedy wing of the Democratic Party. (JAMIE ROSE/GETTY IMAGES)

Ted embraces Barack Obama as Caroline Kennedy looks on, January 2008. Ted and Caroline marshaled the legendary power of the Kennedy name to help boost Obama's presidential candidacy. (EMMANUEL DUNAND/AFP/GETTY IMAGES)

Right: Ted and second wife Victoria relax at their home in Hyannis Port. Unlike Joan, Vicki is a bold personality and more than a match for Ted. (TED FITZGERALD/BOSTON HERALD)

Below: After his seizure, Ted is visited at the hospital by (from left) Patrick, stepson Curran, Teddy Jr., Kara, and Vicki. The atmosphere in his VIP suite began to resemble an Irish wake.

(BILL GREEN/BOSTON GLOBE/LANDOV)

Ted returns to the Senate with Vicki and his Portuguese water dogs after brain surgery. There have been times when his life has seemed a shambles. Yet even then, in the summer of his life, as surely now, in its winter, he was a lion.

(ALEX WONG/
GETTY IMAGES)

PART FIVE

"A Master Legislator"

18

IN 1996, FOLLOWING two years of bitter haggling, Joan announced that she and Ted had reached a revised divorce settlement. Under this agreement, she didn't receive any additional funds. But, she added rather cryptically, she was "now protected in the event of Senator Kennedy's death."[1] Some people interpreted this to mean that Joan would continue to receive alimony payments even if Ted's death preceded hers.

After several more spectacular mishaps, Breathalyzer tests, court-ordered probation, and confinements for alcohol abuse at McLean Hospital in Belmont, Massachusetts, Joan's children decided to take more drastic legal measures. In this, they were encouraged by their father and Vicki, who felt that Joan got kid-glove treatment from everyone because of her frail condition. Kara, Teddy Jr., and Patrick sought—and were granted—legal guardianship of their mother's medical treatment and supervision over her daily affairs.

Judge Robert Terry ruled that Joan was "incapable of taking care of herself by reason of mental illness." The exact nature of her illness was not revealed, but according to a family friend, it referred to Joan's bipolar disorder and depression. "The children are there for her as much as they can be, but she has no husband and no significant other, and she's someone who really needs someone to be with her," said the friend.[2]

"My brother, sister, and I love our mother very much," Patrick said. "She has done so much for us throughout our lives, and we will take whatever steps necessary to ensure she gets the medical treatment and care she needs and deserves. . . . These decisions are never easy, and in our case, all too early in our mother's life."

Joan was sixty-eight years old when Teddy Jr. was chosen by his siblings to be their mother's legal guardian.

As TED KENNEDY approached his seventieth birthday, he began to think more and more about his family's legacy. He had high hopes that his nephew John F. Kennedy Jr. would follow in his footsteps and be the one to fulfill the promise of a Kennedy Restoration. Ted believed that, of the thirty Kennedy cousins in John's generation, only JFK Jr. had the charisma to go all the way to the White House. Thus, in the summer of 1999, Ted met with JFK Jr., who was thirty-eight years old, to discuss his entry into political life. It was Ted's strongly held view that JFK Jr. should set his cap for the New York governor's race in 2002. New York was a solid Democratic state, and the capital of Albany, with its easy access to the financial makers and shakers of Wall Street, would be an ideal launching pad for the presidency.

JFK Jr. was attracted by his uncle's proposition. But he had a serious problem. His marriage to Carolyn Bessette was on the rocks, and divorce seemed a virtual certainty. The brutal publicity stemming from a divorce, as Ted knew from bitter personal experience, was harmful to a political career, and so Ted decided to intervene to save his nephew's marriage.

"New York's archbishop, John Cardinal O'Connor, loved being in the limelight and dealing with important people," said an associate. "At the Kennedy family's request, he got involved and tried to save John's marriage. He acted as a marital mediator with John and Carolyn."

But the cardinal was too late. For on July 16, 1999, John F. Kennedy Jr., along with Carolyn and her sister, Lauren Bessette, took off from a small field in New Jersey after dark in John's Piper Saratoga high-performance plane to attend a wedding on Martha's Vineyard. Within minutes, they disappeared into the roiling fog over Long Island Sound. That was Friday. On Monday, July 19, 1999, the National Oceanic and Atmosphere Administration's vessel *Rude* located the fragments of John's plane off the coast of the Vineyard.

"The divers went in and recovered the human remains," Captain Burt Marsh, the U.S. Navy's supervisor of diving and salvage, told the author of this book. "It took a couple of hours. You can never play down the impact of recovering remains under circumstances like this. No diver likes that idea. It's not their favorite thing."[3]

The retrieval of JFK Jr.'s body—thirty years to the day since Ted Kennedy had driven his car off the bridge on Chappaquiddick Island—revived talk of a Kennedy Curse. It was a shattering experience for John's friends, relatives, and admirers, and the entire country was plunged into a period of mourning. Less noticeable, John's tragic death altered the basic dynamics within the Kennedy family.

To begin with, there was a radical change in the relative wealth of family members. In the 1950s, Joseph P. Kennedy had been listed by *Fortune* as the ninth wealthiest person in America; in today's dollars, he was a billionaire. By the 1990s, however, *Forbes* reported that the Kennedy family "barely qualifies for the Forbes Four Hundred," the magazine's list of the richest Americans. Joe's children—Jean, Eunice, Patricia, and Ted—were worth about $30 million each; *their* children—the so-called Kennedy cousins—were worth far less.[4]

But upon the death of Jacqueline Kennedy Onassis in May 1994, Caroline and John had shared equally in a vast inheritance. This included their mother's fortune (worth an estimated $70 million); Jackie's 366-acre oceanside property on Martha's Vineyard ($50 million); President Kennedy's share of the family trust created by Joe Kennedy ($30 million); their father's Hyannis Port house ($3 million); the proceeds from the family's sale of the Chicago Merchandise Mart and other related properties ($76 million); and the profits from two auctions of family artwork, furniture, and jewelry ($40 million).[5]

At the time of JFK Jr.'s death, he and Caroline were each worth more than $100 million. Caroline and her three children— Rose, Tatiana, and John—were the prime beneficiaries of JFK Jr.'s estate, which effectively doubled Caroline's net worth to more than $200 million. Now, suddenly, Caroline was not only the sole surviving member of Camelot's First Family; she was also by far the richest Kennedy cousin. Her rank in the ambitious and competitive Kennedy clan soared.

Ted had always been crazy about Caroline. And Caroline reciprocated his feelings. It was Uncle Teddy who had walked Caroline down the aisle at her wedding to Edwin Schlossberg, a designer of interactive museum exhibitions, which was held at the Kennedy Compound in 1986. "My brother Jack is here tonight," Ted said at the wedding reception. "He would be so proud of his daughter. He loved her so much." And it was Uncle Teddy who had taken care of the arrangements for JFK Jr.'s cremation and burial at sea, and his funeral, sparing Caroline those gruesome tasks.

Following that funeral, Ted seemed to treat Caroline differently than he did other members of the family. At first, the change was almost imperceptible. But gradually it became apparent that Ted was transferring his political dreams for JFK Jr. to Caroline. When it came to public exposure, Caroline resembled her mother, who had shunned the spotlight. Given Caroline's shy and reclusive nature, she was at first naturally reluctant to pick up the torch dropped by her brother. And yet, she was aware that if she didn't claim the flame, some other Kennedy cousin would step forward and try to take her beloved brother's place.

19

———

In JUNE 2001, the Senate was embroiled in one of the biggest health-care debates in its history. At stake was the Bipartisan Patient Protection Act. The conservative version capped punitive damages at $500,000 in federal court. The liberal version, which was supported by Ted Kennedy, John Edwards, and John McCain, capped damages at ten times that amount—$5 million.

President George W. Bush threatened to veto the Kennedy-Edwards-McCain bill if it landed on his desk.

"The way Ted handled this impasse explains why he is called the Lion of the Senate," said a former White House aide. "Ted invited Josh Bolten, the White House deputy chief of staff; Nicholas Calio, the president's assistant for legislative affairs; and John McCain to his house in the Sheridan-Kalorama neighborhood in D.C. When Ted Kennedy invites you to his house, you go, not because he's a Kennedy, but because he's earned your respect for successfully coauthoring so much legislation with both Democrats and Republicans.

"It was all very informal," this person continued. "Ted greeted us at the door. We sat around the living room. There were only principals, no staff, because Ted knew that staff always takes a hard-core position; they're interested in certain predetermined outcomes. But Ted isn't that way. His rhetoric can be fiery, but he uses it to give him cover in coming to a compromise. And that's what he did that day."[1]

The Senate approved the slightly watered-down Kennedy-Edwards-McCain bill by a vote of 59 to 36, which, thanks to the recent powwow at his home, Ted felt confident President Bush would sign. But he was in for a rude disappointment. The House of Representatives passed a more conservative version, which could not be reconciled in conference with the Senate version.

And so, no bill was ever sent to the president. To a nonpolitician, the outcome could be seen as a loss for Ted Kennedy. But that was not the way it was interpreted by his Senate colleagues. They knew that he had reached across the great divide of party and ideology, that he had not burned any bridges, that he would live to fight another day, and that—what was most important in the halls of the Senate—he had won everyone's respect.

"He's a legislator's legislator," said Senator Jon Kyl, a staunch conservative Republican from Arizona. "At the end of the day, he wants to legislate, he understands how, and he understands compromise."[2]

Learning to settle for half a loaf, Ted had compiled a legislative record unsurpassed by any living senator. Among the scores of bills bearing his name or imprint, he could take credit for the Civil Rights Act of 1964; the Voting Rights Act of 1965; the expansion of the voting franchise to eighteen-year-olds; the 1997 Kennedy-Hatch law providing health insurance to children; the 1982 Voting Rights Act extension; the 1996 Kennedy-Kassebaum bill, which made health insurance portable for workers; the 1998 law that allocated billions for AIDS testing, treatment, and research; the 1990 Americans with Disabilities Act; the 1993 Family and Medical Leave Act; and the 2001 No Child Left Behind Act.

How did Ted evaluate his own record? What did he think of the comparisons that some made between him and the Senate greats of the past—Calhoun, Clay, and Webster?

"I'm finally hitting my stride," he said in his typical self-effacing manner.[3]

The historian Michael Beschloss put it more elegantly during a ceremony in the caucus room of the Russell Senate Office Building, where JFK had announced in 1960 that he'd be a candidate for president.

"I don't need to tell anyone in this room that if you had to choose one of the great historical figures in the U.S. Senate in the past two centuries, Edward Kennedy would be at the top of the list. . . . I often think of President Kennedy, who in the 1950s had to choose some of the great Senators whose portraits would be painted on a wall here on Capitol Hill. I think that if he were to do that today, his brother would be on that wall as a master legislator. . . .

"If you wanted to write the history of America over the last seventy years, you couldn't do better than to study Edward Kennedy's life," Beschloss continued. "Oftentimes the presidency gets more attention than many Senators who have served, and when you have a Senator who has served as Edward Kennedy has served for [more than forty] years, it's a very good example of the fact that . . . a Senator who makes that much impact can do more to change American history than some presidents of the United States."[4]

. . .

. . .

As he grew in political stature, Ted cut back on his drinking and dissociated himself from some of the people he had run with in his salad days. However, there was one person from the past whom he could not ignore: his ex-wife Joan. In the early-morning hours of Tuesday, March 29, 2005, Patrick Kennedy was roused from sleep by a call from his brother, Teddy. Their mother had taken a serious fall. She had been found bleeding on a Beacon Street sidewalk. She was in the hospital with a concussion and a broken shoulder.[5]

Over the next few days, Patrick learned the sad truth about his mother. She had stopped going to Alcoholics Anonymous meetings and had been secretly guzzling mouthwash and vanilla extract. Doctors told Patrick that his mother's drinking had inflicted so much damage on her kidneys that she might need dialysis to stay alive.[6]

"You want to make sure there's someone there for her all the time," Patrick said, "but at the same time you don't want to encroach on her privacy too much. When things like this happen, it makes you feel as though maybe you should have done more to make sure there's someone with her 24/7, and perhaps that might become necessary."[7]

Two days later, Patrick, a six-term Democratic congressman from Rhode Island, announced that he would not follow his father into the Senate. He was dropping plans to challenge Senator Lincoln Chaffee, a Republican, in 2006. "My family means everything to me," Patrick said.

"The ongoing situation that is occurring with his mother has really taken a personal toll on Patrick," said Anthony Marcella, Patrick's former chief of staff. "It has been personally very painful to him. Not only seeing her suffer from this terrible illness, but to do it in such a public way is really tearing him apart."

Even then, however, Patrick and his siblings might have left well enough alone if they hadn't discovered that their mother had secretly transferred the Squaw Island house out of her name and into a trust controlled by her second cousin, Webster Janssen, a person her children didn't know. Janssen had asked Cotton Real Estate of Hyannis to put the house on the market for $6,495,000.

Since their father's marriage to Vicki, the children hadn't felt welcome in the Big House. They considered the Squaw Island house to be *their* home as much as it was their *mother's*. And so, the children took their mother to court, and an acrimonious battle ensued for control of the house. A trial date was set for June 13, 2005, in Barnstable Probate and Family Court to hear the *Kennedy* v. *Kennedy* lawsuit.

"I think they are mean-spirited and vindictive," said Webster Janssen, referring to Joan's children. "And they should get on with their lives and stop badgering poor Joan. . . . She's sort of living under house arrest most of the time."[8]

"Basically," Teddy Jr. replied, "my mother's taking it out on us by trying to sell the house."[9]

In the end, an embarrassing public trial was averted at the last moment when Joan and her children resolved their differences out of court. Under the agreement, the trust established by Janssen was dissolved and the Squaw Island house was taken off the market. In addition, the trial judge appointed a nonfamily guardian to keep an eye on Joan, and also put her fortune, estimated at $9 million, in the hands of a new trust overseen by two court-appointed trustees.

"She is very upset about the whole thing, very stressed out," Janssen told the author of this book. "She can't go anywhere on her own."

Why did Joan Kennedy agree to become a ward of the state? It appeared that, in return for accepting a court-appointed guardian,

Joan obtained the right to sell the Squaw Island house, just as she had wanted to in the first place. And in fact, six months after the out-of-court settlement, Joan put the house back on the market for $6.5 million. Although Ted Kennedy had the right of first refusal, he had assumed a hefty mortgage when he bought Jack's old house in the Compound from Caroline Kennedy, and he didn't have the cash to meet Joan's price. As a result, the house, which the Kennedys had long cherished as part of their heritage, went to a stranger, whose identity remained undisclosed.

"When it came down to it, Joan really had no choice about becoming a ward of the state," said a family friend. "The fact is, she had been threatening suicide, and if she hadn't agreed to a guardian, she could have been institutionalized. This way, at least she'll be able to participate in family gatherings, pursue her interest in music, and take part in various charitable events. That's a lot better than being locked up in a mental institution."[10]

Ted felt sorry for Joan. But, as he told friends, he did not think he was responsible for her problems. They had been divorced for more than two decades, and Joan had to walk her own path. His responsibility, he felt, was to nurture and promote the Kennedy legacy.

In January 2008, Ted endorsed Barack Obama for president of the United States. At the time, it seemed like a risky move. He did not merely express a marginal preference for Barack Obama over Hillary Rodham Clinton, who was then being touted as the overwhelming favorite to win the Democratic Party nomination. In a typically extravagant gesture, he wheeled out his nieces Caroline Kennedy and Maria Shriver to help him anoint Obama as nothing less than the embodiment and personification of his brother John Fitzgerald Kennedy. Like JFK, Barack Obama would "lift our spirits and make us believe again."

Some thought Caroline Kennedy, who was inspired by Obama, had influenced Ted Kennedy in his choice of the charismatic first-term African American senator. But that was only partly true. After all, other Kennedy cousins—such as Bobby Kennedy's children Kathleen Kennedy Townsend, Robert Kennedy Jr., and Kerry Kennedy—were zealous supporters of Hillary Clinton.[11] More important, Ted Kennedy saw himself as the guardian of liberal orthodoxy, the tribune of leftist interest groups—trade unions, feminists, environmentalists, teachers' unions, black activists—that defined the base of the Democratic Party.[12]

Ted believed that, after four decades of cautious-to-conservative administrations under both Republican and Democratic presidents—Nixon, Ford, Carter, Reagan, Bush I, Clinton, and Bush II—the political pendulum was finally swinging back in *his* direction, from Right to Left, and that Barack Obama represented a once-in-a-generation opportunity to restore activist government as the country's dominant public philosophy.

Until now, the United States had experienced only five such political realignments, marking the end to one period of American history and the beginning of another: the election of 1800, in which Vice President Thomas Jefferson defeated President John Adams and ushered in a generation of Democratic-Republican Party rule; the election of 1828, in which Andrew Jackson, the first president not born of privilege, defeated John Quincy Adams; the election of 1860, which brought Abraham Lincoln to the White House and unleashed the forces of the Civil War; the election of 1932, in which Franklin Delano Roosevelt created the coalition that defined the modern Democratic Party; and the election of 1980, in which Ronald Reagan launched a generation of conservative rule.

As Ted Kennedy saw it, with the election of Barack Obama, the long Dark Age in American politics—a period that began with JFK's assassination—would finally draw to an end, and a great liberal awakening would follow. Universal health care would finally become a reality. And America's tattered reputation would be restored throughout the world. Such was the breadth and scope of his confidence in Obama and the future.

Ted's endorsement of Barack Obama was a breathtaking moment in the political life of the country. For it pitted the fabled Kennedy Dynasty, with its vast fund-raising resources, against the powerful and equally well-funded Clintons in a battle for the heart and soul of the Democratic Party. In point of fact, the senator had never wholeheartedly embraced the Clintons. Like most politicians, he had a long memory, and he had never forgotten that the Clintons had worked on behalf of his archrival, Jimmy Carter, at the 1980 Democratic National Convention.

Since then, Ted had grown ever more leery of the Clintons and their efforts, through the centrist Democratic Leadership Council, to distance themselves from the liberal Kennedy wing of the Democratic Party. And so, when Hillary gave an interview during the primary campaign crediting President Lyndon Johnson, rather than John F. Kennedy, for the Voting Rights Act of 1965, Ted Kennedy did not view it as a trivial oversight. It went to the heart of his feelings about his brothers and the cause they had bequeathed him. Ever since his maiden speech in the Senate, on April 9, 1964, the senator had been at pains to lay claim to civil rights as a unique Kennedy legacy.

"No memorial oration or eulogy could more eloquently honor President Kennedy's memory than the earliest possible passage of the civil rights bill for which he fought so long," the senator declared in his maiden speech, his voice choking on his tears. "My brother was the first President of the United States to state publicly that segregation was morally wrong. His heart and his soul are in this bill. If his life and death had a meaning, it was that we should not hate but love one another; we should use our powers not to create conditions of oppression that lead to violence, but conditions of freedom that lead to peace."[13]

Over the years, some dismissed Ted Kennedy's devotion to the cause of civil rights—indeed, his commitment to the poor, the persecuted, the sick, and the mentally ill—as a transparent political stratagem, a cynical way to get votes. Others portrayed him as a hypocrite—a rich man who did not live by the very laws and regulations he prescribed for everyone else. But Ted Kennedy's expressions of empathy with the underdog were more than empty platitudes; his ability to understand and share the feelings of others was woven into the narrative of his life.

SPEECHIFYING ON BEHALF of Barack Obama, Senator Kennedy was a wonder to behold. His arms flailed and flapped, his face turned a brilliant red, and he piled hyperbole on top of hyperbole. At an Obama rally before a friendly Hispanic crowd in Laredo, Texas, the senator broke into an off-key rendition of the Mexican song "Ay Jalisco No Te Jajes" ("Don't Give Up on Me"). Then, with his snow-white hair falling over his forehead, he delivered an electrifying oration, proving again that he remained one of the great stump speakers of his time.

Remarkably, the senator's oratorical style had not changed over all these years. It was still a throwback to the Honey Fitz era of torch-lit parades and grandiloquent speeches. He spoke to crowds as though the microphone had not yet been invented, as though he needed to project his unaided voice to the farthest reaches of the auditorium, and even beyond, into the future itself.

His unmodulated "bellowing," wrote journalist Ron Rosenbaum, "was not Teddy at his best; it was loud, graceless, crude and bombastic, as if he was substituting sheer volume for the kind of charisma and charm his brothers had. . . . Still, when he was speaking—or bellowing—to packed halls filled with partisans, whipping up the faithful even if it seemed over-the-top, *it didn't come across as weird, and in its own way it worked* [italics added]."[14]

And so, whatever one thought of the senator's ideas, and the way he expressed them, he could always be counted on to provide exciting political theater. Shortly after his carotid-artery operation in October 2007, he appeared at a ribbon-cutting ceremony at the New Bedford Whaling National Historical Park.[15] According to those who saw him, he looked better than he had in years.[16]

"His weight was down," wrote *Boston Globe* columnist Kevin Cullen. "He had a bounce in his step, even if he still had that limp. . . . He was energized by the prospect of Barack Obama becoming the Democratic presidential nominee."[17]

20

Hyannis Port, Saturday, May 17, 2008

A T FIRST LIGHT, Sunny and Splash bounced into the senator's bedroom and woke him by licking his fingers. Groggy but obliging, the senator swung his legs over the side of the bed, and, struggling against age and gravity, lifted himself to an erect position—or as nearly erect as his old bones would allow. He threw on some warm clothing, then headed out the door into the chill, salty air for a stroll on the beach with his Portuguese water dogs, who loved to go down to the sea as much as he did.[1]

Early risers among the senator's Cape Cod neighbors watched as he shambled off toward the beach. He was carrying a tennis racket and lobbing balls over the heads of his dogs. Splash easily outran Sunny and won the game of fetch every time.

"Now whaddaya want, now whaddaya want?" The senator was

speaking to Splash. "Good boy, yes, yes—g'boy, g'boy. Gimme the boooll now, gimme the boooll now."

Sunny and Splash were spooked by all the noise at the Kennedy Compound. This morning, workmen were unloading crates of iced clams and setting up a huge party tent and sound equipment for the rock band The B-52s. A couple of hundred guests were expected later in the day for a concert to raise money for Best Buddies International, a charity founded by Anthony Kennedy Shriver, the senator's nephew, to help people with intellectual disabilities. Like the Special Olympics, another Kennedy charity, Best Buddies was dedicated to the memory of Rosemary Kennedy, the senator's mentally disabled eldest sister, who had been lobotomized when Ted was nine years old.

Rosemary's ghost was not the only specter wandering the Kennedy Compound, six acres of lawns that sloped gently down to the sea. Here, many years ago, in the cold waters of Nantucket Sound, the senator's eldest brother, Joe, threw young Teddy overboard for failing to heed a command during a sailing race. Here, on the broad green lawn, John-John and Caroline ran to greet their father as he stepped off the presidential helicopter. Here, on the beach, Bobby walked alone, weighed by grief and guilt, after his brother's assassination. Here, on the verandah of the Big House, Ted's father spent his last years, mute and paralyzed by a stroke—a manifestation of bad karma, and a terrifying example to the senator of how he might end his own days.

"John, campaigning, had Robert to work for him," wrote the historian Garry Wills. "Robert had Edward to advise [him] and be his surrogate. Edward has no one but ghosts at his side. . . ."[2]

The senator lived in the house that his father purchased in 1928 when Hyannis Port was still an out-of-the-way fishermen's village.* Joe and Rose Kennedy gutted the house that first winter, expanding it into fourteen rooms and nine bathrooms to accommodate the eight children they already had plus one more, who would be named after Joe's best friend, Edward Moore. The town remained much as it was in the early years. Towering white clapboard houses clung to the hillocks; privet-lined streets beckoned the town's many children to ride their bikes and play. Most of the eight hundred families had views of the teeming harbor.

Nowadays, the senator slept in his father's old bedroom. He ate in his father's dining room. He entertained in his father's living room, which was dominated by a glass display case containing his parents' collection of two hundred costumed dolls from all over the world and a large oil painting of the destroyer USS *Joseph P. Kennedy Jr.* His father's plan to make young Joe president of the United States perished along with Joe in a plane explosion over the English Channel during World War II. Ted was twelve when Joe Jr. died.

Framed photographs of other young lives cut off at the promise covered the walls, the tables, and the piano. There was a picture of Kathleen Kennedy, the senator's sister, who married the future duke of Devonshire, and who also died in a plane crash. She was twenty-eight at the time; Ted was sixteen. There was a photo of Bobby, who was assassinated when he was forty-two and Ted was thirty-six. There was a portrait of John F. Kennedy Jr., the senator's nephew, whose plane went down in the Atlantic Ocean, claiming the lives of three people—JFK Jr., who was thirty-eight, and his wife and sister-in-law. There were photos of Bobby's sons David and Michael, the

---

*Ted rented the house he had purchased from Caroline to his sister Eunice Kennedy Shriver and her family.

first dead of a drug overdose at twenty-eight, the other as a result of a reckless skiing accident at thirty-nine. . . .

The ghosts of Kennedys Past refused to be still. They roamed the winding lanes of Hyannis Port. They lingered in the village News Shop, which opened on Memorial Day weekend and closed after Labor Day. They floated in the sparkling harbor, which was crammed with a forest of masts, including those of the senator's fifty-foot schooner *Mya*.

"Most of the families in Hyannis Port have had homes here for years and have known the Kennedys, for better or worse, through four generations," said a longtime friend of family matriarch Rose Kennedy, who died in 1995 at the age of one hundred and four. "The Kennedys have influenced nearly every life in Hyannis Port in one way or another. They have had affairs with countless women in the town, both married and single. Some women have had affairs with several members of the clan. There are three women who live within a few blocks of the Compound who have had long-term affairs with Ted. There are families where mothers have had affairs with Kennedy men of their generation and their daughters have been involved with Kennedys of the succeeding generation.

"And all of these multigenerational affairs have made for complicated relations. You have to be careful what you say because you never know who has deep, intimate ties to whom. Just as complicated are men and women who have had business or political relations with the Kennedys. Some people know one set of secrets, others another.

"Nobody who gets into the Kennedys' circle and has entrée to the Compound wants to lose it. So there is a constant jockeying for position. It's like a royal court, replete with intrigue, backstabbing, and toadying. Nobody trusts anybody."[3]

. . .

THIS SATURDAY MORNING, as the fog rolled out to sea, the senator and his dogs headed onto the beach. About a mile away, dimly
visible through the drifting mist, he could make out the shape of the
cottage he had purchased on Squaw Island shortly after hc married
Joan Bennett in 1958.

The senator had once been greatly fond of that rambling, gray-
shingled house called Brambletyde, which sat high atop a hill overlooking Nantucket Sound on one side and a salt marsh on the other.
The house had a long history in Ted's family: his brother Jack first
leased it in the spring of 1963, because the Secret Service thought
the president and his family would be safer there than at the Compound. Joan had loved it, too, and called it "a forever house, a home
we bought to live in our entire lives."[4]

The cottage was now host to its own phantoms. For the house
that Ted and Joan had fought so hard over during their divorce was
now owned by total strangers.

The senator lobbed a tennis ball into the water, and Sunny
dove in after it, easily outswimming Splash. With the ball in his
mouth, Sunny made his way back to shore, shook himself dry, and
ran up to the senator.

"G'boy, g'boy," the senator said. "Gimme the boooll now."

Suddenly, the senator felt his jaw tighten, and then he noticed
his left arm becoming numb.

"Dear God, don't let me go like Pop," he later recalled thinking. He had a horror of having to spend his last years in the same
condition as his paralyzed father—fully conscious, but imprisoned
in a useless body.[5]

He fell to the sand. Staring straight up at the high thin clouds scudding across the New England sky, he realized he could not move. His worst fear had come true: he *was* paralyzed like his father.

Sunny and Splash reacted to their master's collapse with frenzied yelps and barks. Several workmen heard the commotion and came running to the senator's aid. They carried him back to the house and summoned Victoria Reggie Kennedy. When she saw her husband's condition, Vicki let out a scream. Then she grabbed her cell phone and dialed 911.

AT 8:19 a.m., Barnstable County paramedics received an emergency call from 50 Marchant Avenue in Hyannis Port. The famous Kennedy address set off frantic alarms. A patrol car on nearby Scudder Avenue got the first call and arrived at the Kennedy Compound within a few minutes. Many other emergency vehicles, including an ambulance and a car carrying the Barnstable fire chief, quickly followed. The street in front of the Kennedy Compound became so congested that more police had to be called in to direct the emergency traffic.[6]

With great effort, paramedics lifted the three-hundred-ten-pound senator onto a gurney, hooked him up to oxygen, and slid him into the back of the ambulance. Vicki remained by his side, refusing to let go of his hand. She whispered encouraging words to the senator as the motorcade of police cars and emergency vehicles (by now nearly all that were available in Barnstable County) raced down narrow, winding Ocean Avenue, hugging the coast and passing through tourist-clogged Hyannis to Cape Cod Hospital.

"Vicki Kennedy knew in a split second that whatever was happening was grave," reported Lois Romano of the *Washington Post*. "As the wife of one of the most iconic and admired politicians in modern history, she also knew it would play out in public. Knowing the media would be tipped off in minutes because of [her] 911 call, Vicki Kennedy worked her cell phone at her husband's side. Before the ambulance pulled up, she had arranged for the senator to be transported from the Cape to Massachusetts General Hospital, called his senate staff to put in place a crisis-management team, summoned family members, and notified his closest friends."[7]

In the emergency room, the doctors examined the senator for two hours. They were shocked at the sight of his grotesquely deformed back. Only a few people outside the Kennedy family had ever seen the senator's back. Among those was Tom Harkin, the long-serving Democratic senator from Iowa and a close Kennedy friend.

"I'll never forget the time I was in the [Senate] steam room with him," Harkin told Adam Clymer of the *New York Times*. "Have you ever seen his back? Oh, God, it's just something that gives me the shivers. His spinal column comes down like this and it literally goes over about three-quarters of an inch and starts down the other way. I don't know how that son of a bitch stands it. . . . I asked him, I said, 'Well, goddamn, doesn't that hurt?' He said, 'Once in a while if I do something funny . . . it bothers me.' I had never seen a back like that."[8]

After the examination, the doctors at Cape Cod Hospital concluded that the senator had suffered a seizure, a little electrical storm of the brain, rather than a stroke, which kills brain tissue and can lead to permanent paralysis. The senator was put back into the ambulance for the three-minute trip to Barnstable Airport. There, a twin-engine medevac helicopter was standing by, ready to airlift him to Boston.

Despite the doctors' assurances that the senator was stable enough to make the sixty-mile flight without a hitch, he suffered another, smaller seizure en route to Boston.

"Vicki about flipped out," recalled a family friend. "Ted tried to play it down and didn't panic, but Vicki cursed a blue streak, saying the doctors were halfwits and shouldn't have let him go. She was seriously pissed. Obviously she had been under tremendous strain all morning, and that put her over the edge."[9]

In less than an hour, the chopper touched down on the roof of Massachusetts General, where the senator was met by his longtime primary care physician, Dr. Larry Ronan. By now, news of the senator's hospitalization had spread via the Internet, and the hospital released a statement saying the senator was "undergoing a battery of tests to determine the cause of the seizure."

By late afternoon, the senator's condition had stabilized and, with Dr. Ronan's approval, members of the immediate family began to arrive at the hospital. The senator's daughter, Kara, who had been battling lung cancer since 2003, flew up from Maryland. His son Teddy Jr., who had lost a leg to cancer as a child, came from Connecticut. His youngest, Patrick, who suffered from a plethora of health problems, ranging from acute asthma to a noncancerous tumor that had been removed in a delicate operation from his spine, flew in from Rhode Island, where he served as a congressman.

Soon, a dozen or so members of the extended Kennedy family— the senator's friends, aides, political associates, and hangers-on— were all crammed into the hospital room, and the atmosphere in his VIP suite began to resemble that of an Irish wake, or, perhaps more accurately, a scene from one of those medieval paintings that depict the death of a great prince. Should it come now, the senator's death would not be sudden and violent, like the deaths of his three brothers. Rather, it would be like those "good deaths" during the Age of Chivalry, which were performed, in the words of one historian, "as on a stage before many spectators, many auditors attentive to every gesture, to every word, eager for the dying man to show what he is worth. . . ."[10]

I~N~ ~SUCH~ ~A~ solemn setting, the first order of business—and the question on everyone's mind—was: Who would lead the Kennedy family after the senator was gone? Who could take Edward Kennedy's place? The Kennedys being the Kennedys—that is, an Irish clan—the senator reserved the right as the chieftain to decide who should succeed him.

None of his children appeared to be up to the job. Kara, whose cancer was in remission, was not interested in politics; she worked for Very Special Arts, an offshoot of the Special Olympics founded by her aunt Eunice Kennedy Shriver. Although Teddy Jr. had talked about running for a congressional seat in Connecticut, he was a sensitive soul who clearly did not have the stomach for the blood sport of politics. As for Patrick, he had inherited many of his father's less attractive qualities—including a penchant for getting into scrapes while under the influence of alcohol—without having inherited his father's political genius.

The first person who had to be considered a serious candidate for family leadership was Robert F. Kennedy Jr., a well-known conservationist and the third of eleven children born to Ethel and Robert Kennedy. Bobby Jr. suffered from a nonfatal vocal disorder called spasmodic dysphonia, which is caused by the involuntary movement of the larynx. It gave his words a high-pitched, strangled sound, and might hinder his effectiveness as a family spokesperson. More important, Bobby Jr. had devoted his life to the environmental group Riverkeeper and had displayed little interest in other political causes.

Bobby Jr.'s eldest sister, Kathleen Kennedy Townsend, once described by *Time* magazine as "the most promising of the next wave of political Kennedys,"[11] had fumbled her big chance by losing her 2004 bid for governor of Maryland. (Kathleen was not the only Kennedy to lose a political race. In 2002, Mark Shriver, son of Eunice Kennedy Shriver, was defeated in a Democratic primary for a seat in the U.S. House of Representatives.) What's more, it was hard to imagine Kathleen as head of the most prominent Catholic family in America after she had publicly lashed the Catholic Church for being out of touch and "on the wrong track."[12]

That left three Kennedys from three different branches of the family as the most likely heirs apparent: Robert Kennedy's oldest boy, Joseph Kennedy II; the senator's wife, Vicki; and John and Jacqueline Kennedy's daughter, Caroline, the last living member of the Camelot family.

The senator was particularly fond of Caroline. With her thick reddish hair, uninflected speaking voice, and tomboy manners, Caroline resembled Ted's sisters more than she did her own mother, Jacqueline Bouvier Kennedy. And Caroline's biting wit and cool demeanor reminded Ted of his brother Jack. Now fifty-one years old, Caroline was at loose ends. Her children—Rose Kennedy Schlossberg, age twenty; Tatiana Celia Kennedy Schlossberg, eighteen; and John Bouvier Kennedy Schlossberg, fifteen—no longer required her constant attention. There were rumors that her marriage to Edwin Schlossberg, an interactive media designer, was strained, but friends said that Caroline and Ed were more or less contented with their marital arrangement.

Since the death of her brother, JFK Jr., Caroline had become a more visible public presence. She'd helped raise tens of millions of dollars for the New York City public schools. She'd recently made a joint appearance with her Uncle Teddy at the annual Profiles in

Courage award ceremony at the Kennedy Library, where her mere presence was enough to stir nostalgia for Camelot. An intensely private person, Caroline once suffered from a severe case of stage fright, but she'd largely overcome that affliction during her many campaign appearances for Barack Obama. Many people thought Caroline was deeply ambivalent about politics. And perhaps she was. However, she was also devoted to her family's tradition of public service—a devotion that would grow stronger in the coming months with the encouragement of her Uncle Teddy.

Political ambivalence hardly described the attitude of Victoria Reggie Kennedy, who was only four years older than Caroline and was the second serious contender for family leadership. Indeed, Vicki's marriage to the senator sixteen years ago had been a political statement in itself.

"When Ted married Vicki, everything changed in his personal and political life," said a Kennedy family lawyer. "She gave him purpose and focus. He has said many times that she saved his life, and he means it quite literally."[13]

The senator was unaccustomedly introspective when it came to his feelings about Vicki. So many people in his family had been taken from him, he said, that he wondered "whether I'd ever really become as attached and committed as I have to Vicki. . . ." And then he added: "She has made an enormous difference in terms of my own happiness."

Ted's view of Vicki bore a striking resemblance to his idealized version of his mother, who also came from a political family. And, indeed, in many ways Vicki filled the role of the all-controlling Rose Kennedy. Not only had Vicki helped the senator clean up his image when she married him, she had been on his case ever since.

Vicki was the key to the mystery of Ted Kennedy's dramatic metamorphosis, which I had noticed at the long-ago dinner at the

"21" Club. It was Vicki who had helped transform Ted from an agitated, fretful, fugitive figure with so much to hide to a more fully developed human being.

"[Vicki] helps him prep for talk shows, works on his speeches and played a pivotal role in his decision to endorse Barack Obama, whom she's been helping court Catholic votes," wrote Lois Romano of the *Washington Post*. "Her political skills and grace are such that there has been quiet speculation that she could succeed her husband in the Senate one day."[14]

THE HOSPITAL ROOM throbbed with undisguised rivalry between Vicki and Joe Kennedy II, the third serious contender for the mantle of family leader.

Notorious for his "boiling temper and quick anger," Joe descended on the hospital wearing his signature custom-made cowboy boots. As the first-born son of Robert and Ethel Kennedy, Joe was the oldest male Kennedy of his generation, a birthright he never let his siblings and cousins forget. Years ago, when Teddy Jr. contemplated running for the seat in the 8th Congressional District of Massachusetts once held by his Uncle Jack, Joe Kennedy II was "pissed" that his younger cousin even considered running without first consulting him.[15]

In the end, Joe claimed the congressional seat as his own. He held it for several terms, and might have gone on to become governor of Massachusetts if he hadn't been sidelined by personal scandal. First, his former wife, Sheila Rauch Kennedy, wrote a book accusing Joe of trying to bully her into having their twelve-year marriage annulled by the Roman Catholic Church. Then it was revealed that his brother Michael, his campaign manager, was having an affair with his family's teenage babysitter. Joe withdrew from the race and, for the time being at least, from active politics. Since then, he had kept his name politically alive in Massachusetts by running the Citizens Energy Corporation, a company that delivers low-cost heating oil to the poor.

Of all the members of the extended family, Joe had been the most vocal in his opposition to his Uncle Ted's marriage to Vicki. "As the eldest of his generation, Joe led the campaign against Vicki, openly mocking her Louisiana drawl and generally acting as though she was little more than a servant," said a friend of the Kennedy family who was present in the senator's hospital room. "Everybody else took their cues from Joe. He was always the ringleader who decided who was good enough and who wasn't. It had been that way since they were all kids.

"Joe vied with Vicki over who was in charge," this person continued. "He ordered a larger flat-screen television be delivered so they could watch the Red Sox game, and called out to [the restaurant] Legal Seafood, ordering a feast of lobster, clams, and shrimp. Mass General is used to the Kennedys' bluster, but this got over the top. The senator has a very serious, probably life-threatening condition, and his family is throwing a Super Bowl party. The combination of so many famous faces and all the merrymaking disrupted the entire floor. Patients as well as staff were crowding around trying to get a glimpse. One of the head nurses stepped in and spoke with Joe, who told her in no uncertain terms to mind her own business. Then one of his assistants called an administrator of the hospital, who said, basically, that they could do whatever they wanted."[16]

THE COMMOTION GREW louder as more Kennedy family retainers squeezed into the already overcrowded hospital suite to pay their respects to the ailing senator.

"The elephant in the room was the notion of succession," recalled one. "The question was, who was in line to take over for Ted, not just, or necessarily, in his Senate seat but as head of the family? There were a lot of very strong characters in that hospital suite and they are all fiercely competitive. Vicki is seen by all as an interloper and she is deeply resented by Ted's children and many of the nephews. Joe, who sees himself the only serious heir apparent, particularly loathes her control over his uncle and hence the family. Joe inherited his father's ruthless gene. He is nothing if not aggressive. And anybody who tries to get between him and Ted's Senate chair is in for a fight.

"In addition, Joe has long resented Caroline, whom he views as haughty and un-Kennedy-like. Caroline is far and away the richest member of the Kennedy clan. After all, she inherited money from her grandfather, her father, her mother, and her brother. Her fortune is a source of unbridled envy and a favorite subject of teasing by Joe and his brothers—a mild annoyance that Caroline sloughs off with an arch half smile.

"But against the backdrop of Ted's sudden deterioration, Caroline's cousins are suddenly looking at her askance, apparently wondering if she is considering declaring herself the heir to Ted's throne. And Joe is suspicious and envious of the way Ted fawns over Caroline. He, doubtless, worries how much influence she has over him. The strangest thing was how Caroline, Joe, and Vicki avoided making eye contact with each other, as though the flying daggers would wound.

"There is no doubt that what Joe fears most is Ted surviving but being physically and mentally incapacitated. That would let Vicki rule in his name for God knows how long."[17]

21

WITHIN DAYS OF the senator's seizure, dozens of TV satellite trucks were staked out in front of Massachusetts General Hospital. There, the senator's spokeswoman, Stephanie Cutter, announced to the assembled reporters that doctors had found a tumor on the senator's left parietal lobe, a section of the brain that controls speech and the ability to understand language. A preliminary biopsy identified the tumor as a malignant glioma, or incurable brain cancer, and further tests showed that the senator had the most aggressive form of the disease—one that had an average survival rate of only 14.5 months.

"It's in a bad site in his brain," said a New York neurosurgeon who had treated many similar cases. "In the senator's age group, it's an incurable lesion. I'm not aware of anyone over the age of sixty-five who has survived. I'd give him no more than six months to a year to live."[1]

Doctors' predictions about such matters are notoriously inaccurate. In any case, the senator was determined to soldier on. Upon his release from the hospital, he told a group of waiting reporters that he intended to race his fifty-foot Concordia schooner *Mya* in Cape Cod's annual Figawi competition on Memorial Day weekend. Vicki, who was standing by his side when he made this statement, visibly blanched.

"No way, his wife thought, was he going to get stuck out in the bay, with no wind, after undergoing a brain biopsy," reported the *Washington Post*'s Lois Romano. "The forecast called for flat seas and not a whisper of a breeze. Vicki Kennedy wouldn't budge. And then . . . a gust! 'So did you see the wind reports?' he asked her hopefully [on] Saturday morning [May 24]. 'Southwest winds up to twenty-five miles per hour.' She threw up her hands. 'Okay,' she said, 'let's do it.' "[2]

As things turned out, the senator was not up to making the first leg of the race on Saturday. However, on Sunday, May 25, he revived and took the 6:30 A.M. high-speed ferry to Nantucket. That night, he sailed the *Mya* in the final leg of the regatta, making the twenty-mile voyage in two hours and twenty-eight minutes, and coming in second in his division.

"It couldn't be a more beautiful day," he said upon arriving at the dock, wearing a blue windbreaker and a Red Sox cap.

"He was bellowing and screaming on the water," said his friend Senator Chris Dodd. "He was really in his form. We had a lot of fun. . . . It couldn't have been a better day to sail."

"It felt great to be out there today," Senator Kennedy added. "It's always a good day to go sailing."[3]

. . .

. . .

AT FIRST, BRAIN surgery did not appear to be a viable option.

"The tumors have these tentacles," explained Dr. Julian Wu, a neurosurgeon at Tufts New England Medical Center in Boston. "It's kind of like an octopus. You might be able to take out the body [of the] octopus, but there might be little tentacles that grow back."[4]

The senator had a good deal of experience dealing with cancer. When his twelve-year-old son, Teddy Jr., was diagnosed with bone cancer in his right leg, the senator consulted a group of specialists on the boy's treatment. After Teddy Jr.'s leg was amputated, he received two years of an experimental form of chemotherapy. When the senator's daughter, Kara, had what some surgeons deemed inoperable lung cancer, he invited a group of experts to discuss her case. They advised surgery, and Kara was still in remission five years later. And so once again, the senator convened a meeting of experts, a "tumor board."

"The meeting on [Friday] May 30 was extraordinary in at least two ways," wrote Lawrence K. Altman, M.D., the chief medical correspondent at the *New York Times*. "One was the ability of a powerful patient—in this case, a scion of a legendary political family and the chairman of the Senate's health committee—to summon noted consultants to learn about the latest therapy and research findings.

"The second was his efficiency in quickly convening more than a dozen experts from at least six academic centers. Some flew to Boston. Others participated by telephone after receiving pertinent test results and other medical records."[5]

At the May 30 meeting, opinions were divided over the benefit of surgery. According to Dr. Altman, "Some neurosurgeons strongly favored it; two did not."[6] Among those opposing surgery was Dr. Raymond Sawaya, chairman of neurosurgery at Baylor College of Medicine and the M. D. Anderson Cancer Center in Houston. Dr. Sawaya believed that the cancer had spread over a large area and, therefore, that most of it could not be eradicated.

"Tumors in the brain are like real estate," said Reid Thompson, director of neurosurgical oncology at Vanderbilt University in Nashville, Tennessee. "It's all location, location, location."[7]

"No matter what treatment you use," said Dr. Henry Brem of Johns Hopkins Hospital, "it tends to be an aggressive, quickly replicating, quickly growing tumor."[8]

Nonetheless, Dr. Vivek Deshmukh, director of cerebrovascular and endovascular neurosurgery at George Washington University Medical Center, urged the senator to take his chances with the scalpel. "The treatment that has been shown to make the most difference as far as survival is removal of the tumor," Dr. Deshmukh said. "Surgical removal carries the greatest benefit in terms of extending his survival."[9]

And so, on Friday afternoon, the senator put in a call to Dr. Allan Friedman, codirector of the Preston Robert Tisch Brain Tumor Center at Duke University Medical Center. The fifty-nine-year-old doctor was considered by many of his colleagues to be the Mozart of brain surgeons. He was preparing to take off for a long-planned vacation in Canada when his cell phone rang. On the other end of the line was Senator Edward Kennedy, who told the doctor that he had searched the world for the best neurosurgeon to remove his cancerous brain tumor.

"And I want you."[10]

. . .

. . .

THREE DAYS LATER, on Monday, June 2, 2008, after nurses had shaved a square patch on the senator's head, he was wheeled into the icy-cold operating room. There, he was to undergo a procedure, pioneered by Dr. Friedman, called "awake surgery." The doctor reminded the senator that a neurologist, standing on the other side of the anesthesia curtain, would ask him questions or ask him to perform certain tasks to ensure that Dr. Friedman did not cut into critical parts of the brain responsible for language.

The senator was heavily sedated for the first part of the surgery. Dr. Friedman made an incision and pulled back the scalp to expose the bone. He drilled a dime-sized hole in the skull and then inserted a second, larger drill bit. After opening a three-inch hole, he used a scalpel to cut through the dura, the layer of tissue covering the brain. It was at this point, after the senator's skull had been opened, that the anesthesiologist awakened him, and Dr. Friedman began to stimulate the brain with an electrode.

"If the stimulation of the electrode causes any changes in task performance, we know that we touched an important part of the brain," explained Dr. Ania Pollack of the University of Kansas Hospital in Kansas City. "We mark that spot and we know we cannot injure it. That is called cortical mapping."[11]

Peering through a high-powered microscope, and using a computer system to help him navigate the brain, Dr. Friedman began to expose the tumor. Then he used high-frequency sound waves and heat to dissolve the cancerous tissue and suction it out. He tried to remove as much of the tumor as possible, but the disease had cells that were well beyond the visibility of the electron microscope, and the doctor could not root out and destroy all the cells.

Nonetheless, Dr. Friedman was pleased with the results, and he announced that the surgery had "accomplished our goals." Combined with radiation, chemotherapy, and experimental brain-cancer drugs, such as Temodar, Avastin, and a novel vaccine called CDX-110, the senator was expected to survive for several months.

Left unsaid, however, was an inescapable fact: The malignant tumor was already growing back.

22

T ED'S FIRST FEW weeks at home in Hyannis Port were a harrowing experience. His doctors started him on chemotherapy treatments, and for a while he was so drained of color and vitality that he looked as though he was at death's door.

But he was an old hand at wrestling with the Angel of Death. Three of his brothers, a sister, and two nephews had all died violently; he had barely survived a plane crash that took the lives of two people; one of his sons had lost a leg to cancer; his daughter was a lung-cancer survivor; and, of course, Ted bore responsibility for the death of a young woman many years ago.

Despite these dreadful experiences (or perhaps because of them), he refused to succumb to self-pity and despair. As the hellish chemo treatments proceeded, he regained his buoyant and cheerful disposition. To everyone who came to visit him, he had one message: He couldn't wait to get back to campaigning for Barack Obama.

But there was just one hitch. The inauguration of the next president of the United States was still more than seven months away, and Ted Kennedy had been discharged from the hospital with a grim prognosis. Half of all patients with his form of incurable brain cancer—a malignant glioma—died within a year, and those of his advanced age (he was seventy-six years old) usually went a lot faster.

Still, there were days when he felt well enough to be wheeled down the wooden pier of the Hyannis Port Yacht Club for a look at his beloved two-masted schooner, the *Mya*. Ninety-four-year-old Benedict Fitzgerald, who had served as Rose Kennedy's personal attorney until her death, happened to be on the pier that day, and he reeled back in shock when he recognized the frail figure in the wheelchair.

"It was clearly going badly for Ted," Fitzgerald said in an interview for this book. "I have a lot of happy memories of that beach. Many happy days with members of the Kennedy family over the years, dating back to when Joe Kennedy [the family patriarch] bought the place in the nineteen-twenties. But this was one of the saddest days.

"I remember Joe landing in a seaplane when Ted was just a baby," he continued. "Joe had Gloria Swanson with him and a film can under his arm. Joe had had a movie theater built in the basement of the house. They said it was the only private movie theater in New England, and I suspect it was. He had a projectionist and everything.

"Joe invited us all to come and watch his latest movie. Gloria stayed at the house, and Rose was perfectly welcoming. She didn't seem to know or care that this movie star was Joe's mistress.

"When Ted is gone," Fitzgerald added, "the house and all those memories will be history. Rose wanted to turn the place over to the Benedictine monks before she died. I drew up the legal papers for her on my front porch. But when Ted found out about it, he ripped the thing in half. There was no way he was going to have the place turned into a monastery."[1]

ON SUNDAY, JULY 6, 2008, Harry Reid, the Senate majority leader, phoned Vicki Kennedy in Hyannis Port to ask if her cancer-stricken husband was well enough to travel to Washington and make an appearance on the floor of the United States Senate. Just days before, a vote on a critical Medicare bill had fallen one shy of the sixty needed to break a Republican filibuster. Ted's "aye" vote would tip the balance and break the filibuster.

"But," Reid quickly added, "I'm not pushing, just asking."[2]

No one in Hyannis Port wanted Ted to go, not his children, not his doctors, and not the person who ultimately decided such matters—Victoria Reggie Kennedy.[3] But as he gained strength, Ted decided to overrule his wife, children, and doctors and fly to Washington to break the Republican filibuster. On Wednesday, July 9, he traveled to Washington in virtual secrecy; few of his colleagues outside the Democratic leadership knew of his plan to make a surprise appearance on the Senate floor. He did not want to give the Republicans time to plot a counterstrategy.[4]

Just after four o'clock in the afternoon, he showed up at the north wing of the Capitol with Sunny and Splash, his Portuguese water dogs. The guards and the few Senate aides who happened to be passing by were thunderstruck by his appearance. Word quickly spread, and the hall began to fill with photographers and reporters.

For years, reporters assigned to cover Ted Kennedy had carried advance copies of his obituary with them, figuring that if his compulsive eating and drinking did not get him first, some nut with a gun might.[5] But he had defied the odds. Of all the Kennedy brothers, only he had lived long enough, in the words of the Irish poet William Butler Yeats, "to comb grey hair."

And now, like some apparition, he had come back to the Senate, where he had managed to accomplish more than either of his two brothers, John and Robert Kennedy. At present, he was the second-longest-serving member in the United States Senate, after Robert Byrd of West Virginia, and the third-longest-serving since the inaugural session of the Senate back in 1789. His colleagues on Capitol Hill—even those who heaped scorn on his liberal agenda—referred to him as the "Lion of the Senate." They predicted he would go down in history as one of the chamber's greats, up there with Henry Clay, Daniel Webster, and John Calhoun.[6]

He was proud of his mastery of the Senate, and no longer regarded himself as a runner-up in history because of his failed attempts to win the White House.

"I feel the Senate is where the action is," he once explained, "where the great issues of war and peace, the issues of human rights and the problems of poverty are being debated. And, with certain important exceptions, you really *can* get a vote there on important matters. I would say the Senate is the greatest forum for change in our country and in the system. It's the forum that I very much want to be part of and have some influence with."[7]

There were those who would deny him that role. They still viewed him as a relic of the past, a tax-and-spend liberal, an overweight, debauched politician who had left Mary Jo Kopechne for dead at Chappaquiddick; who had been caught making love to a beautiful luncheon companion on the floor of La Brasserie restaurant in Washington, D.C.; who was complicit in a lurid rape case in Palm Beach—who, in short, was beyond the hope of salvation.

However, this caricature was woefully out of date. It had been fifteen years or more since his name had been linked with any scandal. And it had been even longer since he had given serious thought to running for the White House. As a result, he had ceased being a paramount threat to the Republicans. He was no longer the politician so memorably described by the late Republican Party chairman Lee Atwater as "the man in American politics Republicans love to hate."[8] His name was no longer used by conservative political action committees to raise millions in direct-mail advertising.[9] In recent years, the senator's most clamorous critics had fallen silent, or been drowned out by those who believed that Ted Kennedy had atoned for his sins.

The person who best captured this merciful view of the senator was the writer Murray Kempton. "In the arrogance of our conviction that we would have done better than he did in a single case [i.e., Chappaquiddick]," wrote Kempton, "we exempt ourselves from any duty to pay attention to the many cases where he shows himself better than us."[10]

AND SO, ON this fine summer's day, it was fair to say that Ted Kennedy had not merely survived long enough "to comb grey hair," he had prevailed. He was the greatest lawmaker of his age, a trusted member of that small fraternity of men and women who have guided the course of America's destiny.

As his wife and his niece Caroline Kennedy watched from the packed Visitors Gallery, Ted Kennedy was escorted onto the floor of the Senate by his younger son, Congressman Patrick Kennedy, and his friends Senators Barack Obama, John Kerry, and Christopher Dodd. His unheralded appearance caused an instant sensation. Dozens of his colleagues rose to their feet and let out whoops of delight.

He "stirred the normally staid chamber to a rousing ovation and moved many colleagues to tears," reported the *New York Times*.

"Looking steady but flushed . . . Mr. Kennedy was quickly surrounded by Senators who could barely keep from overwhelming him despite cautions to keep their distance because his treatments have weakened his immune system."[11]

The *Jewish Daily Forward* could not contain itself. "There may be no better example than [Ted Kennedy] of how complicated human beings can be," wrote the *Forward*'s Leonard Fein. "Ted Kennedy is very far from sainthood. There have been times when his life has seemed a shambles, earning disgrace. Yet even then, in the summer of his life, as surely now, in its winter, he was a lion. It was Martin Luther King who asked to be remembered as a drum major for justice, for peace, for righteousness. If that were so, he added, 'all the other shallow things will not matter.'

"Ted Kennedy: A drum major for righteous indignation."[12]

Epilogue

—

A HARD FROST set in early on the Cape in the fall of 2008, and Vicki Kennedy feared that the bitter cold would hasten the demise of her desperately sick husband.

"A number of things were going wrong," said a family friend. "Ted was determined to get in every last sail on the *Mya*, but even he had to admit that the weather was foul. The nasty weather depressed him, because he considered every day that he was forced to stare at the sea from his porch to be a bad day, and his days were dwindling quickly."[1]

Ted went back to drinking heavily. Although Vicki tried to keep him away from the hard liquor in the Big House, he had many friends in Hyannis Port who felt sorry for him and who saw no harm in sneaking him a bottle or two. Vicki's father, Judge Edmund Reggie, suggested that they ship the *Mya* to South Florida and move there for the winter. The judge had a friend who owned an estate on Biscayne

Bay in the Miami area, which he had been trying to sell but was having trouble unloading in the depressed real-estate market.

The move was quickly arranged. The *Mya* was shipped south on a flatbed truck. Several boxes of photographs and Kennedy memorabilia followed. Office space was rented near the Biscayne Bay estate so that the senator could set up quarters for a small working staff. Ted's primary care physician, Dr. Larry Ronan, promised to make frequent trips from Mass General in Boston to check in on his famous patient. While Ted was wintering in Florida, the University of Miami's Leonard Miller School of Medicine, which had a world-class center for treating malignant gliomas, agreed to provide any therapy or specialized treatment that Ted might require.

In the days leading up to Ted and Vicki's departure, Ted wandered around the Big House, gesturing at photos of family members, most of them long dead. "It was as though he was familiarizing himself with the faces of those he'd soon be rejoining," said a family friend.[2] Ted also made a point of saying good-bye to everyone who worked in the Kennedy Compound. A lot of these people had been with the Kennedys for years, and he wanted to say his farewells in case he didn't get another chance.

"I'll be back in the spring," he told them, but there wasn't a great deal of conviction in his voice.[3]

From Vicki's point of view, the move to Florida served a dual purpose. Not only would the Florida weather be easier on Ted's delicate health, but the relatively isolated location of the estate also meant that only a handful of people would have access to Ted's address and phone numbers. In Florida, Vicki was able to keep Ted under far tighter control than she could in Hyannis Port.

"He still calls on the holidays," said one of his oldest New York City friends. "I can still make him laugh. But I speak more to Vicki than to him, because it's too difficult. She's cut off most of his historical contacts, people who've been his political supporters for the past forty years, including Jewish supporters in the financial community. She's even regulated his contacts with his immediate family, and his closest friend, John Tunney. I don't think Ted wanted that. But sometimes in a marriage you have to pay a price."[4]

The weather that winter in Florida turned out to be wretched— cold and gloomy—which meant that Ted couldn't go sailing as often as he wanted. When he was trapped indoors, he stayed in touch with John McDonaugh, his chief health care policy adviser, who was aiming to get a Kennedy-crafted health care bill on the floor of the Senate before the July 4 recess. Ted also worked on a long-standing oral history project that would eventually be housed in a wing of the John F. Kennedy Library. He was a first-class anecdotalist, and when a particular story out of his past caught his fancy, he made three copies of the audiotape and sent them to his children.

THERE HAS BEEN a Kennedy in the Senate for more than fifty years—ever since John F. Kennedy's first term—and Ted wanted to extend that run for another fifty years," said a longtime Kennedy family adviser. "He felt it was very important to have a Kennedy in the Senate after he was gone, and when Hillary [Clinton] announced she was leaving the Senate to become secretary of state, Ted thought that Caroline should take her seat. He put it to Caroline almost like a last wish, and Caroline felt that she couldn't let her Uncle Teddy down."[5]

The family adviser who provided this insight into Ted and Caroline's thinking had a unique set of credentials that allowed him to speak with authority about private Kennedy matters. He had been an intimate of the Kennedys since the early days, when Joe and Rose first arrived in Hyannis Port, and he was still in touch with members of several generations of the family, including Ted and Caroline, as well as Caroline's three children, Rose, Tatiana, and Jack.

As might be expected from someone this close to the family, he was delighted at the prospect of a new Kennedy face in the Senate. In early December 2008, Caroline phoned David Paterson, who had replaced the disgraced Eliot Spitzer as governor of New York State, and expressed her interest in the Senate seat vacated by Hillary Clinton. Paterson had the sole authority to name Hillary's successor, but since everyone from New York's Mayor Michael Bloomberg to President-elect Barack Obama supported Caroline's bid, she was considered to be a shoo-in for the post.

However, the new governor didn't seem as impressed by the magical Kennedy name as everyone else, and he let Caroline twist slowly in the wind. While he dithered over his selection, Caroline launched a listening tour of upstate New York that turned into a political disaster of major proportions.

"During a series of meetings with the New York press, one of which was recorded and is now being admired on YouTube in all its ineloquent awkwardness, the daughter of President Kennedy was vague, unconvincing and displayed a potentially ruinous verbal tic," reported the correspondent of *The Times* of London, who, like most of the world press, was covering Caroline's every move. "In one sequence, lasting two minutes and twenty-seven seconds, Ms. Kennedy, fifty-one, revealed that she had inherited none of the eloquence, energy or charisma associated with other members of America's foremost political dynasty: she used the phrase 'you know' no fewer than thirty times."[6]

In early January 2009, Caroline was finally granted a face-to-face interview with David Paterson. But by that time, the New York media (aided and abetted by leaks from Paterson's office) were speculating that the governor might not choose Caroline for the job because she lacked "electoral experience." Worse yet, New York City's competing tabloids, the *Daily News* and the *Post*, were having a field day poking fun at Caroline for the inept rollout of her candidacy, and for her stuttering interjections of "you knows."[7]

"Caroline was humiliated; she had expected that the appointment would automatically be hers," said the Kennedy family adviser. "In her mind, it wasn't just that it had been her uncle Robert's Senate seat, or any other aspect of her legacy; it was that she is a constitutional lawyer who has helped secure funding for the New York City school system, that she's acted as an adviser to her uncle, and that she's a star of the Democratic Party. It honestly never occurred to her that the seat wouldn't be given to her immediately. When Governor Paterson failed to react, and made her wait, she seethed."[8]

Caroline called a number of Democratic power brokers in Washington and Albany, and during those calls, she vented her rage. This was a side of Caroline that few people had ever seen, or even suspected. According to several veteran politicians who took her calls, Caroline sounded like the old Bobby Kennedy—loud, harsh, and grating.

"In the end, her daughters, her son, and her husband, Ed, sat down with her at their New York apartment and gave her something of an ultimatum," said the Kennedy family adviser. "Her children felt that she was becoming a different person—one that they didn't much like. They had never seen her so angry or heard her talk so tough. They told her that if she was getting this worked up just getting the job, they didn't want to see what she would be like in the trenches of a political campaign or a fight in Washington.

"One night, Caroline and Ed Schlossberg were dressing to go out to a dinner party when her daughters, Rose and Tatiana, came into her bedroom to confront her about the situation. Caroline was putting on her makeup and was a few minutes from leaving when they sat down on her bed and told her what they were thinking. When they knew they had her attention, Rose, the eldest, ran out and got her little brother, Jack, to join them so that their mother would know they were unanimous.

"Jack is actually the most emotional of the kids, and he was the most upset. This was totally uncharted territory for them. Mom had always been in charge. Their family is very matrilineal. Caroline calls the shots. Rebellion is not something that happens. For that reason Caroline was stunned. She stopped what she was doing and gave them 100 percent attention, shushing and waving Ed out of the room when he ducked in and pointed to his watch to indicate that they were running late.

"Rose pleaded, saying, 'Mom, you are above this.' That was a wake-up call. It jerked Caroline back to reality. What would *her* mother [Jackie] think of all this tabloid attention she was getting? Her mother wouldn't have liked it. It was Caroline's conversation with her children that tipped the balance. If Paterson had called and offered her the job an hour *earlier,* she would have accepted. But after that conversation, she wouldn't have taken the job if Paterson had come *begging* on his hands and knees. That's when Caroline called Paterson and told him she was withdrawing her name."[9]

CAROLINE'S DECISION CAME as a crushing blow to Ted. And it was quickly followed by several other setbacks.

On January 20, 2009, at a celebratory luncheon on Capitol Hill after the inauguration of Barack Obama, Ted collapsed and had to be rushed by ambulance to a nearby hospital. Doctors attributed his seizure to fatigue, but according to members of his family, he had been drinking heavily the night before. Though Ted seemed to bounce back from the episode, the seizure was a dramatic reminder that, ultimately, he was locked in a losing battle with cancer.

But he was desperate to keep the battle going for as long as possible, and shortly after his collapse in the Capitol, he submitted to experimental medical treatments. Using cells from his brain tumor, doctors created a vaccine that was meant to stimulate his immune system and help him fight the cancer. While he was undergoing these treatments in Florida, researchers in Europe were using other cell samples from Ted's cancer to come up with an alternative vaccine to suppress or shrink the tumor. Such pioneering methods were generally used when all conventional approaches had been exhausted.[10]

The news from Capitol Hill was equally grim. Tom Daschle, President Obama's choice for secretary of health and human services, was forced to withdraw his name after it was learned that he had failed to pay $128,000 in taxes on a car and driver lent to him by a big Democratic donor. The withdrawal of Daschle, who was also set to head a newly created office on White House health reform, devastated Ted Kennedy. He had quit the Judiciary Committee to focus exclusively on his life's great dream—comprehensive health-care reform. His staff had been working round-the-clock to create legislation for passage during the first one hundred days of the new administration. Now, as President Obama set about searching for Daschle's replacement, everything was put on hold, and it was anybody's guess whether Ted would still be around to lead the debate when the bill finally reached the floor of the Senate.[11]

On Monday evening, February 9, 2009, Ted returned to Washington for the first time since Inauguration Day. He went there to cast his vote on President Obama's $838 billion economic recovery package. As he entered the Senate chamber, his colleagues were taken aback by his appearance. His once-luxurious head of snow-white hair had thinned considerably, and his hand trembled when he greeted Senator Max Baucus, the chairman of the Finance Committee, who managed the debate on the stimulus bill.[12]

Ted left immediately after the vote and made his way, with the aid of a cane, to a room where Vicki was waiting for him. In the past several weeks, Vicki's constant presence at Ted's side had added to the speculation that she might succeed her husband in the Senate. If that's what Vicki had in mind, she was in for some stiff competition, for back in Massachusetts, Joe Kennedy was already running a thinly disguised campaign for his uncle's seat via a blitz of TV commercials touting his efforts to deliver low-cost heating oil to the poor.

Vicki helped Ted on with his coat and looped a long blue scarf around his neck. Ted picked up a soft felt fedora hat and squashed it down on his head.

Since the days of JFK, Kennedy men had never liked to wear hats. They thought hats made them look silly. Hats were for sissies. But Ted obviously didn't care anymore about such things. He just wanted to stay warm—and alive. In fact, he'd agreed to submit to another brain operation. "I hope to put it off as long as possible," he told a family friend in late March, "but I'm sure I'll have to go back in for surgery at some point."

As he stepped into the elevator, someone called after him, "Senator, how are you feeling?"

Ted looked up. A small crowd had gathered at the elevator to bid him farewell.

"How are you feeling?" someone in the crowd repeated.

"Some days are better than others," Ted Kennedy replied as he disappeared behind the sliding doors.

ACKNOWLEDGMENTS

—————

THE FOUNDERS OF our country believed that a virtuous nation requires virtuous people to run it. But history has taught us otherwise. In actual practice, virtue has always been in short supply among the world's leaders. Two of the greatest figures from the past were France's Charles de Talleyrand-Périgord and Britain's King Edward VII. Now universally regarded as among the most accomplished statesmen of their time, these men were also devoted to lives of lechery, fornication, and self-gratification. The same can be said of two of America's great nineteenth-century parliamentarians: Kentucky's Henry Clay and Massachusetts's Daniel Webster. As one of their contemporaries, an American politician and wealthy plantation owner by the name of James Hammond, noted, "[T]he very greatest men that have lived have been addicted to loose indulgences with women. It is the besetting sin of the strong, and of the weak also, of our race. Among us now Webster and Clay are notorious for it."[1]

More recently, journalists, historians, and biographers have substituted the psychological notion of "character" for "virtue." They argue that it is necessary to unearth intimate details of a person's life in order to decide whether that person has the "character" to be our leader. But in their search for leaders of character, they have only proved what most of us already knew: that all men (and women, for that matter) are sinners.

These thoughts come to mind when one tries to describe the tangled task of writing a biography of Edward Moore Kennedy, a figure who equals Talleyrand, Edward VII, Webster, and Clay as both public giant and private rogue. How does one explain that despite Chappaquiddick, despite Palm Beach, despite a dozen other lesser transgressions, Ted Kennedy ranks as one of the two or three greatest senators in American history?

One cannot rely on Ted Kennedy to solve the riddle. Following his diagnosis of a malignant brain tumor in May 2008, he stopped giving interviews. Not that it would have made much difference if he had made himself available. Although Ted Kennedy has uttered hundreds of thousands of words during a career that has spanned nearly half a century, he has never spoken candidly about matters close to his heart.

For such insights, a biographer must turn to the senator's friends, associates, and family members, who, if they are willing to talk at all, will do so only on the condition of anonymity. As a result, I owe an enormous debt of gratitude to more than a score of people whom I cannot thank by name. It takes a great deal of courage to speak out of school about a Kennedy, for if you are caught, you will most surely be expelled.

As for those names I can name, let me begin with my longtime research associate Leon Wagener. Many of the gems in this book were unearthed by Leon in his visits to presidential libraries. He also gained the trust of several of Ted's intimate friends, who provided unprecedented fly-on-the-wall scenes of private Kennedy gatherings.

I must thank another longtime associate, Melissa Goldstein, who was the photo editor of this book, as she has been on several other Kennedy books that I have written. By now, Melissa and I have become so familiar with each other's photographic sensibilities that we communicate almost telepathically.

This is the second book of mine that has been edited by Rick Horgan of Crown. Rick shapes a manuscript the way a potter shapes a clay vase—hands-on. For all those who complain that editing is a lost art in the book publishing business, Rick is the artist who disproves the rule. He saved me more than once by helping me rethink the structure of the book, and by guiding me to place greater emphasis on areas of Ted Kennedy's life that might otherwise have been slighted.

Over the course of many proposals, contracts, manuscripts, and finished books, Dan Strone of Trident Media Group has been my constant guide and mentor. He is my agent in the largest sense of that word—a person who acts on my behalf. No more can be asked of a friend.

Many friends provided moral support. Two who deserve special mention are Ronald Kessler and James Abernathy.

Finally, since words won't suffice to thank my wife, I must resort to a simile and compare her to Penelope, the faithful companion of Odysseus, who displayed such patience while her husband was away on a journey. Writing a book is like a long and hazardous journey. It is good to come home again to the woman I love.

SOURCES

ABBREVIATIONS

ACP . . . . Adam Clymer Papers, John F. Kennedy Presidential Library

HJF . . . . Hamilton Jordan Files, Jimmy Carter Presidential Library

HKP . . . . Henry Kissinger Papers, Richard Nixon Presidential Library

HRHP . . . . H. R. Haldeman Papers, Richard Nixon Presidential Library

JCPL/POF . . . . . Press Office F, Jimmy Carter Presidential Library

JCPL/WHCF . . . White House Central File, Jimmy Carter Presidential Library

JEP . . . . John Erlichman Papers, Richard Nixon Presidential Library

RGP . . . . Richard Goodwin Papers, John F. Kennedy Presidential Library

RKP . . . . Rose Kennedy Papers, John F. Kennedy Presidential Library

RWRF . . . . Ronald W. Reagan Files, Ronald Reagan Presidential Library

SEF . . . . Stuart Eizenstat File, Jimmy Carter Presidential Library

SMP . . . . Stephen Smith Papers, John F. Kennedy Presidential Library

TSP . . . . Theodore Sorensen Papers, John F. Kennedy Presidential Library

Nixon Tapes

The following tapes were used in the course of research:

February 1971–July 1971
August 1971–December 1971
January 1972–June 1972
July 1972–October 1972
November 1972–July 1973
    Part I: tapes 33, 388, and 813, November 1972
    Part II: November 1972–December 1972

Author's Interviews

Richard Alan Baker • Gerald Baliles • Morton Blackwell
Tony Blankley • Sue Erikson Bloland • Peter Brown • Pat Buchanan
David Burke • Nicholas Calio • Don Fierce • Jim Flug
David Freeman • Webster Janssen • Elaine Kamarck
Paul Kengor • Ron Kessler • Henry Kissinger • Willie Lincoln
Candace McMurray • Victor Navasky • Larry Nichols
Grover Norquist • Zlad Ojakli • Howard Philips • Dan Rather
Steve Richetti • Donald Ritchie • Charlie Rose • Chris Ruddy
Sudie Schenck • Bernadette Malone Serton • Geoff Shepard
Senator Bob Smith • Stephen M. Smith • James Thurber
R. Emmett Tyrell Jr. • Paul Weyrich • Carter Wrenn

Books Cited in Text

Barber, James David. *The Presidential Character: Predicting Performance in the White House.* 4th ed. Englewood Cliffs, N.J.: Prentice Hall, 1992.

Barzun, Jacques. *From Dawn to Decadence—1500 to the Present: 500 Years of Western Cultural Life.* New York: Perennial, 2001.

Beale, Betty. *Power at Play: A Memoir of Parties, Politicians and the Presidents in My Bedroom.* Washington, D.C.: Regnery Gateway, 1993.

Beschloss, Michael R., ed. *Reaching for Glory: Lyndon Johnson's Secret White House Tapes, 1964–1965.* New York: Simon & Schuster, 2001.

_____. *Taking Charge: The Johnson White House Tapes, 1963–1964.* New York: Simon & Schuster, 1997.

Bradley, Bill. *Time Present, Time Past: A Memoir.* New York: Alfred A. Knopf, 1996.

Bronner, Ethan. *Battle for Justice: How the Bork Nomination Shook America.* New York: Union Square Press, 1989.

Burke, Richard E., with William and Marilyn Hoffer. *The Senator: My Ten Years with Ted Kennedy.* New York: St. Martin's Press, 1992.

Cannon, Lou and Carl M. *Reagan's Disciple: George W. Bush's Troubled Quest for a Presidential Legacy.* New York: Public Affairs, 2008.

Caro, Robert A. *The Years of Lyndon Johnson: Master of the Senate.* New York: Alfred A. Knopf, 2002.

Cecil, David. *The Young Melbourne & Lord M.* London: Phoenix Press, 2001.

Chellis, Marcia. *The Joan Kennedy Story: Living with the Kennedys.* New York: Jove Books, 1985.

Clymer, Adam. *Edward M. Kennedy: A Biography.* New York: William Morrow, 1999.

Collier, Peter, and David Horowitz. *The Kennedys: An American Drama.* San Francisco: Encounter Books, 2002.

Connolly, Neil. *In the Kennedy Kitchen: Recipes and Recollections of a Great American Family.* New York: DK Publishing, 2007.

Crowley, Monica. *Nixon in Winter: His Final Revelations about Diplomacy, Watergate, and Life out of the Arena.* New York: Random House, 1998.

Damore, Leo. *Senatorial Privilege: The Chappaquiddick Cover-Up.* New York: Dell Publishing, 1988.

David, Lester. *Good Ted, Bad Ted: The Two Faces of Edward M. Kennedy.* New York: Birch Lane Press, 1993.

Dobrynin, Anatoly. *In Confidence: Moscow's Ambassador to America's Six Cold War Presidents.* Seattle: University of Washington Press, 1995.

Duby, Georges. *William Marshal: The Flower of Chivalry.* New York: Pantheon Books, 1985.

Gibson, Barbara, and Ted Schwarz. *Rose Kennedy and Her Family: The Best and Worst of Their Lives and Times*. New York: Birch Lane Press, 1995.

Goldberg, Jonah. *Liberal Fascism: The Secret History of the American Left from Mussolini to the Politics of Meaning*. New York: Doubleday, 2007.

Gould, Lewis L. *The Most Exclusive Club: A History of the Modern United States Senate*. New York: Basic Books, 2005.

Halberstam, David. *The Fifties*. New York: Villard Books, 1993.

Haldeman, H. R. *The Haldeman Diaries: Inside the Nixon White House*. New York: G.P. Putnam's Sons, 1994.

Hamilton, Nigel. *JFK: Reckless Youth*. New York: Random House, 1992.

Hersh, Seymour M. *The Dark Side of Camelot*. Boston: Little, Brown & Co., 1997.

Highsmith, Carol M., and Ted Landphair. *Union Station: A Decorative History of Washington's Grand Terminal*. Washington, D.C.: Chelsea Publishing, Inc., 1988.

Hilty, James W. *Robert Kennedy: Brother, Protector*. Philadelphia: Temple University Press, 1997.

Honan, William H. *Ted Kennedy: Profile of a Survivor*. New York: Quadrangle Books, 1972.

Howe, Daniel Walter. *What Hath God Wrought: The Transformation of America, 1815–1848*. New York: Oxford University Press, 2007.

Kelly, Michael. *Things Worth Fighting For: Collected Writings*. New York: Penguin Press, 2004.

Kengor, Paul. *The Crusader: Ronald Reagan and the Fall of Communism*. Los Angeles: Regan, 2006.

Kennedy, Joan. *The Joy of Classical Music: A Guide for You and Your Family*. New York: Nan A. Talese/Doubleday, 1992.

Kennedy, Sheila Rauch. *Shattered Faith: A Woman's Struggle to Stop the Catholic Church from Annulling Her Marriage*. New York: Owl Books, 1998.

Kessler, Ronald. *The Sins of the Father: Joseph P. Kennedy and the Dynasty He Founded*. New York: Warner Books, 1996.

Klein, Edward. *Just Jackie: Her Private Years*. New York: Ballantine Books, 1998.

_____. *The Kennedy Curse.* New York: St. Martin's Press, 2003.

Krock, Arthur. *Memoirs: Sixty Years on the Firing Line.* New York: Funk & Wagnalls, 1968.

Kutler, Stanley I., ed. *Abuse of Power: The New Nixon Tapes.* New York: The Free Press, 1997.

Leamer, Laurence. *The Kennedy Men,* 1901–1963: New York: William Morrow, 2001.

_____. *The Kennedy Women: The Saga of an American Family.* New York: Villard Books, 1994.

Madsen, Axel. Gloria and Joe: *The Star-Crossed Love Affair of Gloria Swanson and Joe Kennedy.* New York: Arbor House/William Morrow, 1988.

Maier, Thomas. *The Kennedys—America's Emerald Kings: A Five-Generation History of the Ultimate Irish-Catholic Family.* New York: Basic Books, 2003.

Martin, Ralph G. *Seeds of Destruction: Joe Kennedy and His Sons.* New York: G.P. Putnam's Sons, 1995.

Matthews, Christopher. *Kennedy and Nixon: The Rivalry That Shaped Postwar America.* New York: Touchstone, 1996.

McGinniss, Joe. *The Last Brother: The Rise and Fall of Teddy Kennedy.* New York: Simon & Schuster, 1993.

Navasky, Victor. *Kennedy Justice.* New York: Atheneum, 1971.

O'Brien, Michael. *John F. Kennedy: A Biography.* New York: Thomas Dunne Books, 2005.

Piereson, James. *Camelot and the Cultural Revolution: How the Assassination of John F. Kennedy Shattered American Liberalism.* New York: Encounter Books, 2007.

Reedy, George. *From the Ward to the White House: The Irish in American Politics.* New York: Charles Scribner's Sons, Macmillan Publishing Company, 1991.

Reeves, Richard. *President Nixon: Alone in the White House.* New York: Touchstone, 2002.

_____. *President Reagan: The Triumph of Imagination.* New York: Simon & Schuster, 2005.

Reeves, Thomas C. *A Question of Character: A Life of John F. Kennedy.* Roseville, CA: Forum/Prima Publishing, 1997.

Remini, Robert V. *Henry Clay: Statesman for the Union.* New York: W. W. Norton, 1991.

Renshon, Stanley A. *The Psychological Assessment of Presidential Candidates.* New York: Routledge, 1998.

Rosen, James. *The Strong Man: John Mitchell and the Secrets of Watergate.* New York: Doubleday, 2008.

Ross, Shelley. *Fall from Grace: Sex, Scandal, and Corruption in American Politics from 1702 to the Present.* New York: Ballantine Books, 1988.

Rudman, Warren B. *Combat: Twelve Years in the U.S. Senate.* New York: Random House, 1996.

Schlesinger, Arthur M., Jr. *Journals: 1952–2000.* New York: Penguin Press, 2007.

Shepard, Geoff. *The Secret Plot to Make Ted Kennedy President: Inside the Real Watergate Conspiracy.* New York: Sentinel, 2008.

Sherrill, Robert. *The Last Kennedy.* New York: Dial Press, 1976.

Sinclair, Barbara. *The Transformation of the U.S. Senate.* Baltimore: Johns Hopkins University Press, 1989.

Smith, Amanda, ed. *Hostage to Fortune: The Letters of Joseph P. Kennedy.* New York: Viking, 2001.

Sorensen, Ted. *Counselor: A Life at the Edge of History.* New York: HarperCollins, 2008.

Stephanopoulos, George. *All Too Human: A Political Education.* Boston: Back Bay Books, 2000.

Strober, Gerald S. and Deborah H. *"Let Us Begin Anew": An Oral History of the Kennedy Presidency.* New York: HarperPerennial, 1993.

Sullivan, Gerald, and Kennedy, Michael. *The Race for the Eighth: The Making of a Presidential Campaign.* Cambridge: Harper & Row, 1987.

Taraborrelli, J. Randy. *Jackie, Ethel, Joan: Women of Camelot.* New York: Warner Books, 2000.

Townsend, Kathleen Kennedy. *Failing America's Faithful: How Today's Churches Are Mixing God with Politics and Losing Their Way.* New York: Grand Central Publishing, 2007.

Ulasewicz, Tony, with Stuart A. McKeever. *The President's Private Eye.* Westport, CT: MACSAM Publishing Company, 1990.

White, Theodore H. *America in Search of Itself: The Making of the President 1956–1980*. New York: Harper & Row, 1982.

_____. *The Making of the President, 1960: A Narrative History of American Politics in Action*. New York: Atheneum Publishers, 1980.

Williams, Wendy, and Robert Whitcomb. *Cape Wind: Money, Celebrity, Class, Politics, and the Battle for Our Energy Future on Nantucket Sound*. New York: Public Affairs, 2007.

Wills, Garry. *The Kennedy Imprisonment: A Meditation on Power*. Boston: Atlantic/Little, Brown & Co., 1981.

Witcover, Jules. *The Year the Dream Died: Revisiting 1968 in America*. New York: Warner Books, 1997.

Zeifman, Jerry. *Without Honor: The Impeachment of President Nixon and the Crimes of Camelot*. New York: Thunder's Mouth Press, 1995.

NOTES

EPIGRAPH

1. www.americanrhetoric.com
   /speeches/tedkennedy1980dnc
   .htm.

AUTHOR'S NOTE

1. Martin, Charles, *Metamorphoses: A New Translation*, New York: W.W. Norton, 2005.
2. Newfield, Jack, "Kennedy Rising," *Playboy*, June 1973.
3. Burke, p. 11.
4. ACP.
5. *Ladies' Home Journal*, June 1970.
6. www.ytedk.com/jfk.htm.

CHAPTER 1

1. Honan, p. 113.
2. David, p. 40.
3. Smith, p. 660.
4. Ibid.
5. Martin, pp. 146–47.
6. Matthews, p. 98.
7. Smith, p. 661.
8. Sorensen, p. 125.
9. O'Brien, p. 263.
10. Matthews, p. 90.
11. Perlstein, Rick, "When Nixon Was Channeled on TV," *Wall Street Journal*, December 6–7, 2008.
12. Ibid.

13. Matthews, p. 91.
14. Sorensen, p. 98.
15. Ibid., pp. 106–7.
16. Cecil, pp. 32–33.
17. Ibid.
18. Schlesinger, pp. 236–37.
19. Martin, p. 161.
20. Cecil, p. 212.
21. McGinniss, p. 204.
22. Martin, p. 164.
23. McGinniss, p. 204.

CHAPTER 2

1. Clymer, p. 10.
2. Kempton, Murray, "A Rose That Survives the Storm," *Newsday*, June 6, 1991.
3. Reedy, p. 48.
4. Martin, pp. 267–68.
5. Clymer, p. 15.
6. Ibid., pp. 15–16.
7. www.time.com/time/magazine/ article/0,9171,940066-3,00.html.
8. Burke, p. 31.
9. Leamer, p. 255.
10. Smith, p. 540.
11. Ibid., p. 699.
12. ACP.
13. Martin, p. 159.
14. Smith, p. xxv.
15. Ibid., p. 569.
16. Ibid., p. 618.
17. Ibid., p. 624.
18. David, p. 32.

19. Gibson, pp. 97–98.
20. RKP.
21. Ibid.
22. Ibid.
23. Ibid.
24. Clymer, p. 563.
25. Interview with anonymous source, April 6, 2008; July 2, 3, 11, 24, 2008.
26. Kennedy, Edward et al., "A Grotesque Portrait of Our Parents," *New York Times*, December 3, 1992.
27. Newfield, Jack, "The Senate's Fighting Liberal," *The Nation*, March 7, 2002.

Chapter 3

1. Sorensen, p. 104.
2. Gould, pp. xii–xiii.
3. Martin, p. 159.
4. Ibid., p. 295.
5. McGinniss, p. 202.
6. Ibid., pp. 202–3.
7. Ibid., pp. 216–17.
8. David, p. 42.

Chapter 4

1. Wills, p. 40.
2. Martin, p. 231.
3. ACP.
4. David, p. 47.
5. Ibid., p. 48.
6. Kennedy, Joan, p. 2.
7. Ibid., p. 13.
8. David, p. 44.
9. Ibid., p. 7.
10. Chellis, p. 22.
11. Ibid., p. 21.

12. David, p. 45.
13. Ibid.
14. ACP.
15. Ibid.
16. Ibid.
17. Ibid.
18. Leamer, *The Kennedy Men*, p. 387.
19. Ibid.
20. Ibid.
21. ACP.
22. Leamer, *The Kennedy Men*, p. 388.
23. Ibid.
24. Martin, p. 235.
25. Chellis, p. 25.
26. Taraborrelli, p. 88.
27. Martin, p. 234.
28. Leamer, *The Kennedy Men*, p. 399.
29. Ibid., p. 400.
30. ACP.
31. Ibid.

Chapter 5

1. Martin, p. 267.
2. ACP.
3. Ibid.
4. Martin, p. 245.
5. Ibid.
6. Ibid.
7. David, p. 67.
8. Ibid.
9. Ibid.
10. ACP.
11. Martin, p. 395.
12. Ibid.
13. Ibid.
14. ACP.
15. Ibid.
16. Ibid.
17. David, p. 72.
18. Ibid., p. 73.

19. Clymer, p. 37.
20. Ibid., p. 41.
21. Rick Atkinson, "Why Ted Kennedy Can't Stand Still," *Washington Post,* April 29, 1990.
22. *Time,* December 7, 1998.

CHAPTER 6

1. Martin, p. 457.
2. Ibid.
3. Ibid., p. 458.
4. Ibid., p. 457.
5. Ibid.
6. Ibid., p. 459.
7. Ibid.
8. Ibid., p. 471.
9. Ibid.
10. Piereson, pp. 28–29.
11. Martin, p. 440.
12. Ibid.
13. Klein, *Just Jackie,* p. 122.
14. Barzun, pp. 764–65.
15. Ibid., p. 204.
16. Ibid., p. 781.
17. Howe, p. 514.

CHAPTER 7

1. McGinniss, p. 375.
2. Ibid., p. 498.
3. Ibid.
4. Martin, p. 498.
5. McGinniss, pp. 380–81.
6. Martin, p. 498.
7. Ibid., pp. 498–99.
8. Ibid., p. 499.
9. Ibid.
10. Ibid., p. 499.

11. Ibid., pp. 499–500.
12. Beschloss, *Reaching for Glory,* p. 445.

CHAPTER 8

1. Klein, *Kennedy Curse,* p. 24.
2. Klein, *Just Jackie,* p. 154ff.
3. McCardle, Dorothy, "Ted Kennedy's New Home Is a $750,000 Inside Story," *Washington Post,* March 3, 1968.
4. Martin, p. 534.
5. ACP.
6. David, p. 98.
7. Chellis, pp. 36–37.

CHAPTER 9

1. ACP.
2. Clymer, p. 114.
3. extras.berkshireeagle.com/NeBe/kennedy/default.asp?filename=gray&adfile=ads1.
4. www.americanrhetoric.com/speeches/ekennedytributetorfk.html.
5. David, p. 184.
6. Honan, p. 133.
7. Clymer, p. 124.
8. Ibid., p. 125.
9. Honan, p. 130.
10. Ibid., pp. 130–31.
11. www.muskiefoundation.org/stories.hyman.html.
12. *Look,* March 4, 1969.

CHAPTER 10

1. Clymer, p. 133.
2. Collier, p. 329.

3. McGinniss, p. 577.
4. Clymer, p. 143.
5. Hersh, Burton, "The Thousand Days of Edward M. Kennedy," *Esquire*, February 1972.
6. ACP.

Chapter 11

1. Hersh, Burton, "Thousand Days."
2. Damore, p. 65.
3. ACP.
4. Hersh, "Thousand Days."
5. Damore, pp. 73–75.
6. Ibid.
7. Sherrill, p. 75.
8. Damore, pp. 73–75.
9. Ibid.
10. Ibid.
11. Ibid.
12. Ibid.
13. Ibid.
14. "Inquest into the Death of Mary Jo Kopechne," Commonwealth of Massachusetts, Edgartown District Court. New York: EVR Productions, 1970.
15. Damore, pp. 73–75.
16. Ibid.
17. "Inquest."
18. Ibid.
19. ACP.
20. Ibid.
21. "Inquest."
22. Interview with anonymous source, June 10, 2008.
23. Ibid.

Chapter 12

1. ACP.
2. Honan, pp. 130–31.

3. Ibid.
4. ACP.
5. David, p. 158.
6. Honan, pp. 130–31.

Chapter 13

1. HRHP.
2. JEP.
3. HRHP.
4. JEP.
5. HRHP.
6. Ibid.
7. JEP.
8. Ulasewicz, p. 219.
9. HRHP.
10. Nixon Tapes.

Chapter 14

1. Interview with anonymous source, June 10, 2008.
2. ACP.
3. Ibid.
4. Ibid.

Chapter 15

1. Clymer, p. 247.
2. Schlesinger, pp. 236–37.
3. JCPL/WHCF.
4. ACP.
5. JCPL/WHCF.
6. Ibid.
7. HJF.
8. Clymer, p. 277.
9. ACP.
10. Ibid.
11. Ibid.
12. Ibid.
13. Ibid.
14. Ibid.

15. Ibid.
16. www.americanrhetoric.com/ speeches/tedkennedy1980dnc .htm.

CHAPTER 16

1. ACP.
2. Chellis, p. 247.
3. Ibid., p. 272.
4. Ibid.
5. Ibid., p. 275.
6. ACP.
7. Clymer, pp. 385–86.
8. Ibid., p. 385.
9. Wills, p. 295.
10. Clymer, p. 353.
11. Interview with anonymous source, June 10, 2008.
12. Author's interview with anonymous source, June 10, 2008.
13. Interview with anonymous source, April 7, 2008.
14. Interview with anonymous source, April 6, 2008; July 2, 3, 11, 24, 2008.
15. ACP.

CHAPTER 17

1. Interview with anonymous source, June 10, 2008.
2. Interview with anonymous source, May 30, 2008; June 14, 2008.
3. Clymer, p. 246.
4. Ibid.
5. Interview with anonymous source, June 10, 2008.
6. Ibid.
7. Interview with anonymous source, May 16, 2008.
8. Clymer, p. 247.

9. David, p. 254.
10. Atkinson, "Why Ted Kennedy Can't Stand Still," *Washington Post*, April 29, 1990.
11. Jack Newfield, "The Senate's Fighting Liberal," *The Nation*, March 25, 2002.
12. Ibid.
13. Ibid.
14. Atkinson, "Why Ted Kennedy Can't Stand Still," *Washington Post*, April 29, 1990.
15. Ibid.
16. Ibid.
17. Ibid.

CHAPTER 18

1. Fee, Gayle, and Laura Rposa, "New Divorce Settlement for Joan K," *Boston Herald*, June 26, 1996.
2. Interview with anonymous source, June 15, 2008.
3. www.pbs.org/wgbh/amex kennedyspeopleevents/l_wealth.
4. Clymer, p. 252.
5. Saul, Michael, "Caroline Kennedy: The $100M Woman," nydaily news.com, February 11, 2009.

CHAPTER 19

1. Interview with anonymous source.
2. Rushing, J. Taylor, "Where Right Sees Bogeyman, GOP Sens. See Go-To-Guy," thehill.com, May 21, 2008.
3. Atkinson, "Why Ted Kennedy Can't Stand Still," *Washington Post*, April 29, 1990.
4. Beschloss, Michael, remarks on

launch of Edward M. Kennedy Oral History Project, December 6, 2004.

5. Levenson, Michael, "Joan Kennedy Hurt in Fall; Son Won't Seek Senate," *Boston Globe*, March 31, 2005.

6. Wedge, Dave, and Michele McPhee, "The Fall of Joan," *Boston* magazine, August 2005.

7. Ibid.

8. Interview with Webster Janssen, May 1, 2008.

9. Eagan, Margery, "Joan K's Tragic Saga Plays Out in Public," *Boston Herald*, June 12, 2005.

10. Interview with anonymous source, March 10, 2008.

11. Brown, Carrie Budoff, "Kennedy Family Split on Endorsements," *The Politico*, December 17, 2007.

12. Kelly, Michael, "A Sober Look at Ted Kennedy," *GQ*, 1990.

13. Clymer, p. 57.

14. www.observer.com/node44680.

15. *Huffington Post*, May 5, 2008.

16. Cullen, Kevin, "Always a Fighter," *Boston Globe*, May 18, 2008.

17. Ibid.

CHAPTER 20

1. The description of EMK's awakening on the morning of May 17, 2008, is based on an interview with one of his nephews, who requested anonymity.

2. David, p. 12.

3. Interview with anonymous source, October 2008.

4. Clymer, p. 34.

5. Ted Kennedy described the physical sensations that accompanied his seizure and the thoughts that went through his mind to his nephew Joseph Kennedy Jr., who visited the senator in the hospital within a few hours of the event.

6. Interview with anonymous source, May 19, 2008.

7. Romano, Lois, "The Steadfast Wind in the Senator's Sails," *Washington Post*, May 30, 2008.

8. ACP.

9. Vicki Kennedy's "over the edge" behavior was recounted by Ted Kennedy to the relatives who visited him in the hospital directly after his seizure.

10. Duby, pp. 4–5.

11. *Time*, August 2, 1999.

12. www.absoluteastronomy.com/topics/kathleen_kennedy _townsevd.

13. Interview with anonymous source, April 7, 2008.

14. Romano, "The Steadfast Wind in the Senator's Sails," *Washington Post*, May 30, 2008.

15. Sullivan, p. 24.

16. Interview with anonymous source, April 7, 2008.

17. Ibid.

CHAPTER 21

1. Interview with anonymous source, July 6, 2008.

2. Romano, Lois, "The Steadfast Wind in the Senator's Sails," *Washington Post*, May 30, 2008.

3. Abel, David, "Smooth Sail for Kennedy and Crew," *Boston Globe*, May 27, 2008.

4. McCormick, Cynthia, "Falmouth Family Faces Same Battle as Kennedy's," capecodonline.com, July 24, 2008.

5. Altman, Lawrence K., "The Story behind Kennedy's Surgery," *New York Times*, July 29, 2008.

6. Ibid.

7. Cortez, Michelle Fay, and Tom Randall, "Kennedy's Surgery May Give Doctors Options to Try New Medicines," Bloomberg.com, June 3, 2008.

8. Lynn, Kellye, "Hopkins Doctor Consulted in Kennedy Case," wjz .com, June 4, 2008.

9. Strickland, Eliza, "Ted Kennedy Goes Under the Knife," Health & Medicine, Mind & Brain, *Discover*, June 2, 2008.

10. Collins, Kristin, "Kennedy Chose Mozart of Brain Surgeons," *(Raleigh) News & Observer*, June 29, 2008.

11. Fox, Maggie, "Wide-Awake Brain Surgery Requires Special Care," Reuters, June 2, 2008.

Chapter 22

1. Interview with Benedict Fitzgerald, July 20, 2008.

2. CNN.com, July 9, 2008.

3. Ibid.

4. Hulse, Carl, and Robert Pear, "Kennedy Returns to Help Pass Medicare Bill," *New York Times*, July 10, 2008.

5. David, p. 199.

6. "An Honor Role of Master Legislators," *New York Times*, May 25, 2008.

7. Honan, pp. 113–14.

8. Atkinson, "Why Ted Kennedy Can't Stand Still," *Washington Post*, April 29, 1990.

9. Raum, Tom, "Ailing Kennedy Fading as Top Target for Right Wing," Associated Press, May 30, 2008.

10. Clymer, p. 353.

11. Hulse, "Kennedy Returns to Help Pass Medicare Bill," *New York Times*, July 10, 2008.

12. Fein, Leonard, "A Drum Major for Righteous Indignation," *Jewish Daily Forward*, July 17, 2008.

Epilogue

1. Interview with anonymous source, July 12, 2008.

2. Ibid.

3. Ibid.

4. Interview with anonymous source, January 14, 2009.

5. Interview with anonymous source, January 22, 2009.

6. *The Times* of London, December 30, 2008.

7. Lovett, Kenneth, "Caroline Kennedy Interviewed by Gov. Paterson for Hillary's Senate Seat," nydailynews.com, February 16, 2009.

8. Ibid.

9. Ibid.

10. Allison, Lynn, "Ted Resting after Secret Procedure," *National Enquirer*, February 16, 2009.

11. Weisman, Jonathan; Laura
Meckler; and Naftali Bendavid,
"Obama on Defense as Daschle
Withdraws," *Wall Street Journal,*
February 4, 2009.
12. Cillizza, Chris, "White House
Cheat Sheet: The Hard Math on
the Senate Vote," Washingtonpost
.com, February 10, 2009.

ACKNOWLEDGMENTS

1. Remini, p. 252.

INDEX

Index

6/09